ONCE A REFUGEE

ONCE A REFUGEE

By Christine Gegner and Frid E. Nutley

Seattle   Hawthorne & Peabody   2017

Cover design by Antoneta Wotringer.
Book copyright © 1995 Frid Eileen Nutley.
All rights reserved. This edition was first published in 2017.
ISBN-13: 978-0-9639313-0-6

For Norbert
and dedicated to the memory of
Gunther and Kurt

.

Foreword

I met Christine Gegner in 1977. Attracted by her German accent, I asked her to tell me about her life. As she spoke of her dramatic escape from her Yugoslavian homeland, I said, "Christine, we should write a book!" And so we began what was for Christine a bittersweet experience, as she searched her memory for details long buried. In order to give readers a fuller sense of history as it affected the Gegner family, I enlarged upon her recollections by supplying perspectives on Yugoslavia, Hungary, and Czechoslovakia, as well as on significant military campaigns. We finished the story in 1982, and Christine Gegner died in September, 1993.

Frid E. Nutley
Seattle, WA
September, 1994

CONTENTS

*"If you had known in this day, even you,
the things which make for peace! But now
they have been hidden from your eyes." (Luke 19:42)*

Chapter One

My Collapsing World

For more than two weeks the wagons had been rumbling through our town. Loaded with human misery, they were coming from the east where Germany's front was continuously being forced back by advancing Russian troops. I was very much afraid as I watched from the front window of our home, and I fought the growing dread that what they said could never happen was indeed taking place. Already most of the professional people–doctors, teachers, lawyers, especially politicians–those who had the contacts and money had fled. Yes, the blackest day in Cservenka's history was dawning.

It was early October, 1944. Until a few weeks ago, my husband and I and our three young sons had lived in relative comfort and security in our town in northern Yugoslavia. Although we had quartered troops in our house since the Allied invasion at Normandy in June, the war, I kept telling myself, could not possibly reach our beautiful countryside. Rumors, only rumors. Like the Swiss, we had not interfered with anyone; we were not anyone's enemy. "Who's going to take over our country?" was the question naively asked by many of us. We in northern Yugoslavia really were not a part of the war at all. We just wanted to be left alone to continue our peaceful, prosperous lives.

Left alone. How ironic those words sounded now. I was left alone, all right. Karl was gone–I did not know where. In fact, all able-bodied men in our town were gone. Only old men, women and children remained, left to the mercy of retreating troops and frantic refugees. And my home . . .

For the past two days I had stayed in our quarters with the boys. I kept us together in the front area of the house because I was scared

1

nearly out of my wits by the chaos in my house and in the streets outside. My lovely home was overrun by Hitler's troops, and, although they had been respectful in earlier months, I was now afraid, especially for myself and my maid, two women alone with so many frustrated men caught up in the panic of retreat and a lost cause.

Along with the troops came hordes of German-speaking people, running for their lives from a Russian front which had pushed through Rumania to the Yugoslav border. For nearly two hundred years, German-speaking people had been settlers along the Danube River and its tributaries in Hungary, Yugoslavia, Rumania, Bulgaria, even the Ukraine. *Volksdeutsche* we were called, but though we kept our German language and culture, we were not a part of the Third Reich and its war—or so I thought.

On and on, day after day, and night after night rolled the somber caravan—a sharp contrast to the bright, crisp, sunshiny days of autumn, with the purples, blues, and golds of late-blooming wild flowers and the newly-harvested fields and fruit orchards of the peaceful, fertile *Goldene Batschka*. I loved the sound of the name: *Goldene Batschka*. It spoke not only of the area of Yugoslavia where we lived, but also of its character: golden in terms of its lush productivity, in particular, the acre upon acre of grain swaying to the playful breezes of late summer and autumn. Clashing now with the pastoral setting was the confusion and disbelief that marked the faces of the intruders who were trying to fit themselves in among the few possessions they had had time to grab and load onto their animal-drawn carts, the retreating German troops having already taken all cars, trucks, oil and gasoline.

"What kind of future lies ahead?" I asked myself, as I watched the seemingly endless procession. "We will be safe; surely we won't have to run. It can't happen to us."

Only last spring, Hitler was sending school children into our country because we had everything while Germany lived with rationing. Our German community encouraged us to take them in and give them free room and board. After all, we were all Germans, weren't we? Two boys, one from Austria and one from Westphalia in western Germany, stayed with us. In September, however, with the growing intensity of the war on both fronts, the request came for the youngsters to return to their parents. We loaded ours with as much food from our *Speisekammer* (food cooler) as they could carry. All the while, the German troops who used our house to rest their horses and check their ammunition as they passed to and from the Eastern Front continued to warn us that the day would come when we too would have to leave. But still we would not believe it. We were not doing anyone any harm; why should we go?

My lack of interest in politics, I know now, clouded my understanding. Despite Hitler's swallowing of the Sudetenland in 1938 and his inflammatory speeches claiming that all ethnic Germans owed their allegiance to the *Vaterland*, the thought never crossed my mind that Hitler was deliberately exploiting our sympathy for our German ancestry. Not only that, I paid even less attention to the civil war in southern Yugoslavia. There Tito was struggling to unite the different ethnic and religious groups in an effort to drive out all invading Fascists and to form his own brand of communist state.

In the midst of such international upheaval, my only world was Cservenka. I had never lived anywhere else nor had I traveled farther than to Belgrade, fifty miles away. Cservenka! Is there another place on earth so beautiful?

* * * * *

In my mind I was a little girl again, giggling as my father bounced me on his knee playing "horsey." The youngest of twelve children and born after the others were mostly grown and had families of their own, I was the spoiled darling of my father. By the time I came along, he was semi-retired from farm work and served as *Bürgermeister* (mayor) of Cservenka. To my brother Josef, he had handed over the management of the farm, which was leased to others who lived there rent free and worked in the fields. In return, my father received half the crops. So we had two homes: one at the farm, where I spent most of my early days, and one in Cservenka, about twelve miles away.

I loved the farm, especially the linden tree with its sweet-smelling blossoms, where I had a little tree house. I would sit there by the hour, watching a pair of partridges and their brood of seven. I considered all birds to be my special friends, even the pheasants. Those pests annoyed my father by destroying crops, but they were so pretty that I hated to see them be killed. In the evenings, before we had electricity, my parents and I often sat out on the porch, listening to the crickets or singing songs of our land. My favorite was about a pretty flower, *Kornblumen*, a blue star with white points inside and three blooms on each stem. At times, we would also sing hymns about God's love. My parents had clear singing voices and I always looked forward to those evenings when I had them all to myself. I was glad to be the baby and receive all their attention.

Our land was rich and most Germans were hard workers, so there were no poor people among us. My father grew wheat, corn, oats, and hay—a waving ocean when viewed at harvest from the mountain we had to cross to get to Cservenka with a wagon.

Actually, it was a hill, but to me it seemed like a mountain: very steep, dusty, barren, with no trees or even big rocks, only loose dirt and dust several inches deep, hot and dry in the summer when we had no rain, covered with ice and snow in the winter. I always wondered why such a treacherous place was picked for a road. The climbing up was safe enough, and the view from the top was breathtaking. The descent, though, was scary and I didn't like it. In summer, wagons made their way very slowly, braking heavily. If a load broke loose, the wagon and its load would be destroyed and people who were in the way, injured or maybe killed. In winter, we would go by sleigh, all bundled up in blankets and with hot bricks to keep our feet warm. On the top, my father would stop to attach a braking device to the runners on the sleigh.

Being on top of that hill in winter was like being in another world: pure, silent, stark, majestic, as, in every direction as far as one could see, life lay as dead beneath a winding sheet of nature. But not for long could death imprison life. Each spring, nature burst forth once more, nourished by the very shroud which dared to hold it and becoming as many worlds as there are different shades of green or colors in the rainbow.

Yes, it was safer to go on horseback without a wagon, as we could then travel through the fields and avoid completely the danger of the mountain. Yet without the risk, I would forever have missed the vision of those other worlds.

In addition to the grain fields, my father also had a vineyard, where he grew several kinds of grapes and made wine. It was within walking distance of Cservenka and I would often meet my father there after school so I could pick and eat huge clusters of big, purple grapes.

The path to the fields, however, lay beside swampland where

cattails grew. The place was a favorite of lizards, and in summer I was usually barefooted. Gingerly I would make my way along the quarter-mile-long path, my heart thumping as I dared them to scurry out from among the reeds. They always accepted my dare. Sometimes, when I would wear shoes and get one trapped underfoot, the silly lizard would pull away leaving its wiggling tail to taunt me further. I knew they were harmless, yet I dreaded those lizards.

My reward, though, was the Ox-eye grape, big as crabapples. Even one was too big to eat all at once. So I would first break the skin and carefully suck some of the joice. Then, opening as wide as I could and working my mouth around a grape, I'd tease myself as to the best moment to crush the fruit, and almost choke as the rich juice gushed down my throat. I ate and ate, until I could hold no more. Near the rows of grapes was a region containing dugouts for chilling the wine barrels. It was a safe place for children and I liked being there away from the lizards and the other animals which roamed in the wilder world only a few yards away, up some damp moss-covered brick steps. Beyond them were orchards, a favorite hideaway, I was certain, of wild rabbits, snakes, and porcupines. Not much sunshine filtered through those fruit trees and I was afraid to approach even the steps which led there. Later, at dusk, when I heard the crickets begin to sing "time to go home now," I would take my father's hand and together we walked home, back through the swampland with its lizards. But I was not afraid with him there.

Winter brought another kind of play land: snow, sleds, sleighing, horses with bells. For adults, the severe winters meant hardship, but not for me. All was still, clean, white, beautiful, and carefree.

When I started school, the balance was gradually tipped toward Cservenka, with only my weekends spent on the farm. Sometimes, when my parents were delayed at the farm, on Monday mornings I would have to go to Cservenka for school all by myself. Yet not quite by myself. My horse, Saika, took me. The dark brown animal with its greying muzzle was so tame and faithful that all my parents had to do was place me on her broad, bare back (only adults used saddles), and she would carry me the twelve miles and stop directly in front of our house. After school an old neighbor lady cared for me until my parents came, and I would often sit spellbound as I watched her clicking needles make such pretty things from string and yarn.

Life in the town was not as carefree as on the farm, but I was growing up and found that the town had attractions of its own, in particular, King Alexander Canal. People came from all over every day during the summer to swim. Every year, the canal was emptied of water and cleaned. In a way, I guess the park-like setting reminded me of the country and the special sounds from my babyhood, such as the soothing croaking of the frogs along the banks and the chirping of the crickets. I loved to watch the boats continually moving up and down our canal, which furnished a waterway into the Danube River, and I would dream of places far away—places where those boats could take me . . . far away . . .

* * * * *

I shuddered, as the nightmare flashed across my conscience.

"Why kill innocent Jewish people?" I had asked, aghast, when I heard what was taking place. "These people are our friends and neighbors, born here the same as we. They speak German. And don't we worship the same God?"

First, it was the Morrises, a dear, old couple with a "mom and pop" grocery store. Very pleasant and a little shy, they usually sat outside their store on nice days. They were shot!

Then Mr. Feldman . . . he was shot, too, but his gentile wife was spared.

"Who is responsible for such senseless slaughter?" I had cried. It was incredible that open murder was happening in Cservenka.

The Feldmans had been well-known to our family for years. In fact, Anna, Mrs. Feldman, was related through marriage to my husband's sister. And Mr. Feldman was in the same kind of business. Although competitors of a sort, our rivalry was never bitter. He owned and operated a large silo and, along with us Gegners, would bid on grain. Because we owned a flour mill, we did our own grinding. He, on the other hand, would sell to mills in other towns. There was enough to go around and we all made good livings.

I remember running an errand to his house one day when I was a young girl. My father owed him some money, and I agreed to carry it to him. He was not a big man, but I was afraid of him, probably because he was always finely dressed in a suit and tie. He lived on a street of stately row houses, built out flush with the sidewalk. Timidly, I reached out and pressed the button which rang the bell, then stood back to watch, a queasy feeling in my stomach. I heard the inner door open which let to the entry way and to the door in front of me.

"Too late now," I sighed, as the door opened and he stood before me. Smiling his recognition, he politely invited me in. My stomach relaxed. At the conclusion of our business, he put his hands on my shoulders and looked straight into my eyes.

"Kristina," he said, again smiling warmly, "you are a good girl." All fear melted, and from that day, through all the years, whenever we would pass on the street, he would always, as was his custom, bow and raise his hat.

Three bridges spanned our beautiful canal. Two were drawbridges. The third one, *Die Hohe Brücke* (The High Bridge), was a suspension high enough for ships to pass under. When I was a child, I used to walk across that bridge every day on my way to school. Now horror replaced the happy memories of the times I had skipped carefree over it. *Die Hohe Brücke* had become a gallows, the waters below a grave. There Mr. Feldman met his end.

The Jewish families who owned and operated a sugar corporation in town were also taken to the bridge. All our Jewish people, about twenty, plus a few others—non-Jews who interfered and tried to stop the crimes—were murdered. An evil wind was blowing across Cservenka. Where was it coming from?

Then, a few days ago, right here from this window . . . O dear God! Is the world going mad?

Our wide, two-lane main street had suddenly become one-way, leading north and west, out of town and eventually out of Yugoslavia. One lane was for retreating troops only, the other for fleeing refugees. Now, it appeared, a third lane, the sidewalk, was to be reserved . . . for Jews.

Driven in a bunch of about fifty, all on foot and probably from somewhere in eastern Yugoslavia (for they could not have walked farther), trudged able-bodied men clad only in underclothing, pajamas, or wrapped in blankets. They must have been rounded up at night. I saw no babies, no old people, no women: only young, strong men being herded like cattle by Nazis barking obscene commands. Whenever whips connected with human flesh, there would be a cry—a weak cry—from a body which probably had not eaten for days.

"They're shooting Jews on top of the hill" was the explanation I was given for there being only younger men in this parade. Those who could not keep up with the quickening pace were relieved from having to take another step . . . on the hill outside our town. For even if it meant his own troops went hungry or were left stranded in a military maneuver, the Chosen were not ignored by Hitler. As we were to learn later, the extermination of Jews took precedence over the safety, yes, even over the feeding of his own troops. Therefore, now, although in retreat, German troops still pursued that gruesome goal.[1] A slammed door gave me a jolt, welcomed this time because it let my conscience escape an uneasy moral probing I was reluctant to face. The boys, restless from being confined for two days, were clamoring for something to eat, so I made my way cautiously to the kitchen.

Until a few days ago, eight-year-old Gunther and his brother Kurt, two years younger, had been able to play occasionally in the yard. Even now, with the whole town in near panic, boys will still be boys, and for them, I suppose, the entire scene was rather exciting. They no longer went to school; it had been closed for several weeks. They had spent most of their time following after the retreating soldiers and playing in the big hole in the backyard, the hole which became mud whenever it rained.

"I don't care who gets my nice things; I won't put them in a dirty hole," I had stubbornly promised myself. I could not imagine a sillier order.

A couple weeks earlier, as rumors grew more persistent about a possible evacuation of Cservenka, we were strongly urged to make air raid shelters in our yards for storing our valuables—"just in case Cservenka is bombed." My, how the dirt did fly! Frantic people began digging up their yards to form what looked like walk-in vaults and lining them as best they could with boards to prevent their collapse and to slow the ooze of mud. Then box after box filled with silver, china, crystal, fine linen and damask were carefully placed inside.

The physical effort seemed to give psychological relief, at least temporarily. The rationale given by town officials was that our troubles would be over before we knew it, and even though the next few weeks might prove dangerous, Germany, we were assured, would be victorious: "A breakthrough in missile weaponry is imminent, and as the enemy will be powerless against it, they will immediately sue for peace."

Although history recorded another outcome of the war, that straw of hope was what many were looking for, and they proceeded to line their nests. Then, at night, those who *had*, stole from those who had more!

We, too, dug our hole, but that was all. My life consisted mainly of nice things, and my goal was to get even more. However, if we actually were bombed, I reasoned, would there be any houses to welcome our return to our muddied treasures? I also wondered what our status would be if Germany did win the war. Were we not officially against Germany?

Such were my thoughts as I entered the kitchen, which was no longer my own. Our "guests" helped themselves to whatever food they could find, so I reluctantly joined them and grabbed some bread, cheese, sausage, and milk. Fortunately for us, our larders still had plenty of food. Because we lived in a fertile area of Europe, we always had enough to eat. Even now food was not rationed. All of this had added to our belief that the valleys of the Danube would be held at all costs.

"Held by whom?" I questioned myself, giving in momentarily to a political reality. Yugoslavia no longer had a functioning government. We were partially occupied by the Nazis; the rest of the country was being led by Tito, a Communist, who had the support of the Allies; and our king was in exile for safe keeping. "Whichever way the war goes," I mused as I returned to our quarters with the food, "what will it mean for Yugoslavia's *Volksdeutsche*?" Our speaking German did not automatically make us supporters of Hitler's Reich. We had a cultural sympathy with Germany, it is true, and many were attracted to Hitler's Youth Program. But others firmly held back from full support of a dictator. And even though we Germans had not had complete political freedom under Yugoslavia's monarchs, those who agreed with the principles of a free market feared Communism and its way of forced collectivism. I began to wonder if we might be losers no matter what final course the war took.

At dusk, I put the boys to bed, again in their day clothes. Except for two-year-old Norbert, who was still in diapers, we all slept in our clothes. Clothing piled up everywhere. I did no washing and we ate uncooked whatever was at hand. So even though our words denied that we would flee our homes, our actions belied them.

Animals, though, could not fend for themselves. So a married couple who worked for us were tossing out sacks of feed to our household pets and the chickens, geese, and ducks, getting things settled for the night, when I returned to the window which faced the main street of our town and resumed my watch. More covered wagons . . . wagons . . . wagons . . .

As daylight slowly faded, the never-ending column began to take on a shadowy aspect. Only the grinding wheels, the clomping hooves, and the heaving of horses forced to walk day and night gave life to the ghostly scene. Like a giant pall thrown over the caravan, the gathering darkness muffled all conversation, save for a child's whine, a baby's cry, or an occasional "Whoa."

With sharp reports from the hill, I froze. Not everyone had quit for the day. In an effort to blot a grisly picture from my imagination, I steeled myself to think about Karl.

"Whose guns is he hearing?" I muttered out loud. "The Germans'? The Allies'? And at which front?"

About a month had passed since my husband left. He was part of the *Volkssturm* (Home Guard), composed mostly of older, physically-able men who were not used in combat except in extreme emergency. In the fall of 1940, he had been sent to Zagreb, about fifty miles south of the Austrian border in western Yugoslavia, to fulfill a military training session he had missed in his earlier years, a time he spent traveling around the world. Following our occupation, we had no army fighting under the flag of Yugoslavia. Yet a few weeks ago the order came for Karl, now forty-two years old, to serve. When he left, he did not know where he was going.

At the end of August, however, a new government had come to power in Rumania, which simultaneously had ended its hostilities against Russia and declared war against Germany. Rumania had oil fields vital to Germany's cause. I wondered if Karl had been sent there.

During the ten years of our idyllic marriage, Karl had spoiled me. I had everything I wanted—a beautiful, big house, servants, plenty of money, three fine sons. I did not have to work very hard—in fact, Karl wouldn't let me—and I didn't have a worry in the world. Life just went on. But 1944 brought a change to all that. Not only was October, 1944 a turning point in our personal lives, but those few October days were the prelude to the close of an epoch: the virtual end of the *Volksdeutsche* of Yugoslavia.

If riches increase, do not set your heart upon them (Psalm 62:10).
For the love of money is a root of all sorts of evil, and some
by longing for it have wandered away from the faith . . . . (1 Timothy 6:10)

Chapter Two

German Roots in Yugoslavia

In the 1700s, my great, great grandparents came from Mühlacker in Donautal (the Danube Valley), located between Stuttgart and Karlsruhe in south-central Germany. With thousands of others, they came in answer to a call issued by Maria Theresa, Empress of Austria, as she maneuvered to maintain her territories in the declining years of the Hapsburg dynasty. Her invitation was for people to homestead and cultivate the swamplands of the Danube River basin. My people, mostly Lutheran and religious, settled along the waterway they loved in what was then southern Hungary.

Sturdy, diligent workers, they labored long and hard in their struggle to fill in the swamps, fighting all the while to survive the insect-infested waters, daily risking their lives to typhoid fever, which was rampant in that environment. In return for their sacrifice, they were allowed to live tax free on the land.

Decades of determined work transformed the area into rich, flat farmland. The land grew so fruitful that it became a much fought-over prize, its fields supplying food for much of Europe. Then, as a political plum of Europe's wars of recent centuries, in retribution, our territory was often plucked away from one rule and handed over to another. Therefore, in the several drawings of the map of Europe, the area of the Batschka where we lived was, successively, part of the Austrian Empire, then the Kingdom of Hungary, and from 1871 until the end of World War I, Austria-Hungary. Those alignments, though, at least made sense in terms of nationality, in that our ties with the German language and culture remained intact.

However, when treaty makers again redrew eastern Europe

11

following the "war to end all wars," our status changed. That settlement, sometimes call the "peace to end all peace," lumped together people with dissimilar cultures. In our case, the treaty called for part of the fertile Banat settled by Germans to go to Rumania, and for the western Banat and Batschka where we lived, together with the Slavic districts of Bosnia and Herzegovina of southern Austria and Hungary, to be joined to Serbia and Montenegro to form the Kingdom of Serbs, Croats, and Slovenes, later called Yugoslavia. And so it happened that overnight the several hundred thousand *Volksdeutsche* of Austria-Hungary became part of a newly-formed Slavic nation.

World War II, then, a scant twenty years later, caught us in the awkward position of bearing arms against our German-speaking brothers in support of our new nation–a nation made up of separate states unified in name only and comprising neighbors who spoke Slavic languages. Not only that, two alphabets were used, Roman and Cyrillic, which intensified the rifts geographically and between Roman and Eastern Orthodox Catholics. Also, many Muslims remained from the days when the Ottoman Empire ruled the entire area in the 1500s. Therefore, what we call *nationalism*–a common heritage, a common language, common ideals and ways of looking at life, common institutions and a sense of belonging–was missing.

It was during the First World War, in 1915, that I was born to Jacob and Anna Köhler. My two oldest brothers did not come back from the war, and two children had died in infancy, so I never knew any of them. Three sisters were already married, and shortly after the war three other siblings moved to the United States. So except for the brothers who helped work the farm, I was alone with my parents.

Our town, Cservenka, with its 13,000 inhabitants, served the adjacent farming community by means of its two main industries: a sugar factory and two flour mills. For decades, farmers had brought their beets to the sugar factory and their grain to the flour mills to be processed and shipped to markets in western Europe. Little food was shipped south, as the Slavic peoples were poor and could not compete economically with their wealthier neighbors to the north. In addition, the political and cultural cleavage between them and their northern neighbors led the Slavs quite naturally to favor dealings with brother Slavs to the east. This established pattern did not change even after we were joined politically into one nation.

What I know of those early years, though, was that we lived peacefully under the Yugoslavian government. Apparently happy but poor, many Serbs lived primitively as shepherds and did not farm the land as we did. I remember that our family often gave fruit and vegetables to families living on the hillside around Cservenka. In general, however, we left each other alone: we spoke our language, and they spoke theirs.

When I went to school, however, it was a different story. I was in the third grade the day the order came forbidding children to speak in German. We were told we could not even speak German at home with our parents. From that day, we were to change to the Serbian language.

What a furor that order raised. My parents were too old to change, and traditions ran deep. Had the Serbians proposed a less abrupt plan, the change-over might have succeeded in time, with bilingual children forming the bridge. And in time, I suppose, cultural patterns might also have merged as people intermarried or were otherwise assimilated into a Slavic majority. At any rate, that is the way it usually works with immigrating ethnic groups. But by the 1920s, the *Volksdeutsche* of Yugoslavia were hardly immigrants. And so the plan did not work. The government soon gave up trying to enforce its order and we continued to use our German language.

However, from that time we were increasingly *undertrückt* (suppressed). We governed ourselves—as I mentioned, my father was the mayor of our town—yet we *Volksdeutche* did not have a significant voice in directing Yugoslavia's political policies on a national scale. So we often longed for our fellow Germans in Germany, because we felt they had a kind of freedom which we were being denied. In retrospect, however, it was probably a case of greener grass, but at the time, we did sense a type of isolation in which we were a nation unto ourselves without total power to govern. King Alexander, in his language decree, had tried to bind us together, but the differences were too great to be overcome easily.

And so my upbringing was that of a German farm girl. From the time I was seven years old, I knew what it was to get up at three o'clock in the morning to help set the dough for homemade bread.

"Well, now," my mother would say, "you have to learn. When you are big, you never know when you'll need that. You just get up." And I had to stay side by side with her, next to the great wooden vat, mixing the dough. Sometimes I would fall asleep on my feet, I was so tired. But she would nudge me, gently scolding me to keep awake. By six o'clock, the eight loaves of bread, which would last us about three weeks, went into the oven. When they were gone, we had to start all over again.

At harvest time, my mother always did all the baking for the people who worked for us. Those days were especially busy, and my parents did not have time to entertain me. Our surroundings were not luxurious, but we never lacked for food. Our cycle consisted of gardening, planting carrots and cabbage which, in the fall, we made into sauerkraut. We slaughtered our own pigs and made salami; we had our own cows and made butter, cheese, and buttermilk.

There was no such thing as a refrigerator, so to preserve these dairy products, we had a dark cellar. As a little girl I was afraid to go down there to get butter because I did not even have a light to carry with me. It was not only the dark I feared, though, but some of the creatures I had met there: a huge frog with bulging eyes, and a few garden snakes. I liked to listen to frogs croaking in the distance, but meeting one face to face was another matter. And snakes? Ugh!

"Who is going to eat you up?" my mother would tease. "Nobody wants you. You just go down there and don't be afraid." So I went. But I still shiver when I think about it.

Cleaning also followed a ritual in our German home: Monday was wash day, Tuesday was ironing day, and so on through every day of the week. And I was in on every phase of the cleaning. I remember Mother would give all the furniture, even the wooden floors, the glove test. Whenever she found a speck of dust, I had to start all over again. My protests were greeted by her ever-ready reply: "Now listen, you have to learn to do it right, because when you are older, you never know when you might need it. You just have to learn to do it right."

"You never know when you might need it!" Little did either of us imagine the circumstances which would prove her admonition.

I also learned the "right" way to hang out area rugs and pound them to get the dust out. Then, every Saturday, we washed the windows and scrubbed the floors. We even scrubbed the sidewalks leading to every entrance to the house, and the house itself got a whitewash every two or three weeks.

In all of these cleaning activities, I learned to look forward to

Sunday, because on that day I did not have to clean. My mother used to say, "*Sonntag ist des Herrn Tag. Da ein jeder ruhen mag von aller seiner Arbeit.*" (Sunday is the Lord's Day. Then everyone can rest from all his labors.) We never worked on a Sunday, but since all of us had to put on our best clothes, during the week I had to prepare my starched aprons, my starched blouse, and my skirt. Our clothing was not fancy, but it was clean. Everything was clean. Even the barn was clean.

I thought I was a Christian because my mother and father taught me the right way to live: be good to one another; respect other people's property; do not lie, cheat, or steal. We prayed sometimes and sang Christian songs.

"Oh, there is a God and we are all going to Heaven some day. I'm good enough, so what else is there to do?" Such was the idea I grew up with. I accepted some Christian values, but I did not really know the Lord God.

My family was Nazarene, not Lutheran in the tradition of their German forefathers. In our town, the Nazarenes did not use a church building, choosing rather to meet in homes. While growing up, however, I went to the Lutheran church because at that time there were more young people there than among the Nazarenes. Then, at age twelve, I was confirmed Lutheran. I know my mother did not approve. She had agreed, maybe even vowed, to raise her children as Nazarenes, so she could not give her consent for me to be baptized Lutheran, which must precede classes for confirmation. My father, on the other hand, with the intense social pressures of his job as mayor, was having problems living a disciplined Christian life. This created tension in our home, and it is possible that in arguing with my mother, he gave his permission.

However it was, each Tuesday morning before regular school began we met for confirmation classes. I can yet picture Pastor Sigmund Keck, small and thin, wearing a black robe and white collar with a golden cross hanging around his neck . . . and carrying a cane. He was very strict, especially about silence in the church. Whenever we would giggle or whisper while he was preaching Sunday mornings, on the following Tuesday we would be admonished by Scripture, which he would bang into us with some not-too-gentle taps of his cane on the tops of our heads: "But be ye doers of the word and not hearers only" was one of his favorites. We had a healthy fear of the man as well as a great respect for his honest, sincere life.

In a sense, it was through his church that I met the one who would become my husband. I liked to sing and would go there to choir practice with a distant relative of the Gegner family. I think she was a matchmaker, because it seemed to me that she went out of her way to arrange for Karl to come to the church after practice to walk her home. But then she made quite a point about getting him introduced to me and he ended up walking *me* home. She was an impish dickens about marriage arrangements. Still single herself at thirty-four, she enjoyed helping others make a good match. And here was cousin Karl, thirty-one years old and one of the richest, most eligible bachelors in town.

I knew about the Gegner family—they owned two flour mills, not just one. As the Gegners were far beyond our class socially, it was not likely that a match would be struck between us—even if I did have long, blond hair and was considered pretty. Besides, I liked Peter. Closer to my own age, slender, dark and romantic, Peter endeared himself to me by calling me his *Kristinchen* (little Kristina)—the name my father had used when I was very young. Once, when walking me home, he got up enough nerve to kiss me—right on the cheek! From that time I had a crush on Peter and thought perhaps he would ask me to marry him. And I would have said Yes. He was not at all like the one I had recently refused.

Shortly after my father died, when I was eighteen, a certain insistent suitor came. He was an only child, spoiled and arrogant, and always swinging around in his trench coat. As I could not tolerate him, I would find any excuse I could to be out of the house when he came to call. One time, when I returned from getting my mother some special water at the artisan well a few blocks from our house, I spied him in the living room. I was so determined to avoid him that I crawled into the house through my bedroom window. My plan, however, was not successful. Mother had grown worried when it grew dark and I still had not returned and called out for me. I was forced to answer her call, but I feigned surprise to find a guest waiting to see me.

"Oh, why don't you give up and go home?" was what I wanted to say, but my good manners restrained me and instead I ignored him. I was not gracious, but I did not like him and he never seemed to take a hint. That was the evening he made his proposal.

"I would like to bathe you in milk and honey if you only will accept me, Fraulein Kristina," he purred while bowing. What a braggart. That was too much.

"But I don't want to get married," I blurted out. "And especially not to you!" I added, to myself.

A few months later, though, when I met Peter, it was different. I could love Peter. But what does it mean to have Karl Gegner walk a starched farm girl home from choir practice one week and return the next week to drive her home on his motorcycle? I was not sure. And neither were the townspeople, including Peter.

Karl was tall, handsome, and rich . . . very rich. I knew astonished eyes were watching from behind closed curtains as I rode beside him on the sidecar of his motorcycle.

"What is Gegner Karl doing here?" buzzed from the lips of many jealous neighbor girls. "Seeing Kristina?" They were as surprised as I was. Determined and sure of himself, he was attracted to me, I think, because I was an innocent. The oldest of twelve children, Karl had left home after his own mother had died of blood poisoning at the birth of the last child and his father had remarried. Karl and his stepmother had some differences, so instead of going on to college after he finished high school, Karl traveled around the world for several years, ten of them in the United States, so he spoke fluent English. He had been back in Cservenka only a few months when he began calling on me. His father was ill, and it was expected that Karl would settle down and take over the business.

Therefore, his courting was serious—not romantic, but serious. Within a few days, gifts began arriving: a gold necklace and a gold watch. I felt worthy, a self-worth I had not before experienced that someone of his standing would give me such gifts. I knew my mother was eager to see me married and well cared for so that she could die in peace. This was much on her mind after my father had been killed in a street accident. He was brutally trampled and died within a few hours when he apparently frightened some horses pulling a wagon. Mother was not well herself and was afraid she too would soon die. Her premonition proved true.

"Well," she said, when she heard of Karl's intentions, "this is a good party, and you are going to marry him." I thought, "If Mother says so, it must be right," but as I was not in love with him, I only half-heartedly agreed to the engagement.

"Mama, he's so old. I don't want to get married. I want to go out with others." I was still thinking about Peter.

"What? You said Yes and now you want to go out? Kristina, aren't you ashamed of yourself?"

So I obeyed my mother and married Karl. Within two weeks of our first meeting, we announced our engagement. And to avoid friction with our families, we thought it best not to use the Lutheran church for the wedding. The Gegners were also Nazarenes; Karl's father, in fact, was a lay preacher in the fellowship. Since the setting did not matter at all to Karl and me, we planned a simple ceremony and two months later, at the Justice of the Peace, we were married. Following the taking of vows in December 1934, we drove in our DeSoto car to the Croatian Banat, spending our two-week honeymoon at a luxurious mountain resort.

From that time, my life changed completely. From an innocent farm girl, I became a lady. My husband would not allow me to do any work. I was to be his wife, nothing else. He provided everything.

As a wedding gift, I moved into a brand new brick home Karl's father presented to us. Not only that, but the land on which the house was built contained several oak trees. Some were cut down, and from them we had oak furniture made–for the bedroom, living room, dining room, bathroom, all kinds of pieces in heavy oak, all hand-polished. I had never seen such beautiful furniture. And on the floor were rich, wool carpets, not the few area rugs I had learned how to beat.

I no longer worked in the fields, I no longer scrubbed floors or even dusted furniture, I no longer did the heavy wash. I did do some of the cooking, because I enjoyed cooking and often the help did not follow directions very well. But the maids took care of everything else. My transition from farm girl to lady was soon complete–except in one area.

"You already have ducks, geese, and chickens," Karl chided. "Why in the world do you want more animals? Go out and buy what you need. I don't want to see my wife working in a barnyard."

I had been used to hard work and now, as a "lady," I had too little to keep me busy. Most townspeople, it is true, did not have animals other than household pets such as dogs and cats. But they lived in row houses and did not have land space for them. We, on the other hand, lived on a corner and owned several acres of the surrounding property. In fact, we had about a hundred fruit trees. So I kept on pleading and at last, tired of my nagging, Karl gave in, surprising me one day with a Swiss breed show cow, white and yellow and shiny as a fish. I was delighted. Later, when our boys began to toddle around, Karl agreed to a fluffy, young lamb for each of them. It was comical to watch them play and roll around together, and as they all grew, eventually to see the boys ride them.

With all my free time, though, I grew curious about things and would ask my husband about the possibility of traveling—there were places I wanted to visit.

"Oh, I saw that a long time ago," Karl would reply, and that ended it. So I soon stopped asking; after all, he gave me every material comfort I could ask for. Yet the more we had, the more I wanted, and the result was that instead of being thankful, I grew proud. As a consequence, Karl and I seldom went to church. We were doing very well on our own; who needed the Lord? In the midst of my wealth, I ignored God.

My mother, in the meantime, grew steadily weaker and sadder. I know she prayed for me and that she had encouraged my marriage to a Gegner because they were Christian people and she wanted that for me. But Karl and I were too busy. She died shortly after our first son, Gunther, was born. A huge growth in her abdomen took her life. It might have been cancerous, but few in those days paid much attention to the cause of death. Karl's father, however, did not see his second generation.

"O *Kristinchen*," he would say, when he knew I was pregnant, "I wish I would live long enough to see your first child, and I hope it's a boy." The Gegners had more boys than girls, and of his twelve, eight were boys. Still he wanted another Gegner to carry the name. He died in August and Gunther was born in December. Two years later, we had another boy, Kurt. Gunther was fine-featured; Kurt was a butterball—bouncy, sturdy, strong.

Then we heard Germany was at war and that we, now Yugoslavians legally, were at war with the land of our forefathers, whose language and culture were still ours. Throughout the war, our nation was officially anti-Germany, except for a brief episode when Yugoslav regent Prince Paul (brother of assassinated King Alexander) and his ministers committed Yugoslavia to the Axis. That happened 25 March 1941 and lasted exactly two days. Then, in a successful coup d'etat in Belgrade, a group of Yugoslav Army officers overthrew the pro-fascist government and declared young Peter II, then seventeen years old, to be of age. I remember the action so angered Hitler that he delayed his ambitious invasion of Russia, took over Yugoslavia, and helped his Axis partner, Italy, to conquer Greece. By April 17 Yugoslavia was subdued. The Batschka went to Hungary; the Banat and Serbia were put under German military administration. King Peter, however, escaped to London, where he set up a government in exile.

At that point, resistance sprang up within our nation. First, the Chetniks, led by Draza Mihailovich, started an open revolt against Germany as early as May 10. They fought alone until July, when Hitler doublecrossed Stalin and broke their Moscow Pact of 1939 by invading Russia. Then the Yugoslav Communists, led by General Secretary Tito, quickly joined the Chetniks against a common enemy. However, with their divided allegiance—Mihailovich for the monarchy and Tito for revolutionary Socialism—they were soon fighting each other as well as the Axis, which meant civil war and foreign war at the same time. These actions, though, took place mainly in southern Yugoslavia and not where we lived.

As for Hitler, his breach of the Moscow Pact is considered by many to be the turning point in the war. In one case, his action allowed the Communists to start fighting back, especially in France where they had been effectively stopped from opposing the Germans when they overran the country in 1940. Then too, by invading Russia, he committed his own troops to suicidal maneuvers. The next two years would see also the split of the Axis itself as Italy capitulated and joined the Allies.

Yet despite what was taking place elsewhere, and even despite the fact that since August 1941 all of us in northern Yugoslavia had been under foreign military administration, for several years many of us in Cservenka hardly knew a war was going on, and in 1942 our third son, Norbert, was born. Those undisturbed days were now gone, and the reality was quite plain: the funeral procession ever moving down the street.

I curled up in a chair and threw a blanket around myself, hoping that a few hours of sleep would give me strength to face another day.

"Yet there is no sleep for those outside in the street," I reminded myself. By midnight, however, exhaustion overtook me and I dozed for two hours. Those two hours were the last two hours I slept in my Cservenka home.

He rules by His might forever;
His eyes keep watch on the nations;
Let not the rebellious exalt themselves. (Psalm 66:7)

Chapter Three

Run! . . . Destination Unknown

At two o'clock in the morning, on 8 October 1944, the order came.

"Cservenka must be evacuated by six a.m.!"

To the insistent beat of a drum, the solo voice of the town crier began the chant. What started as a ripple several blocks from our house in the center of town was picked up by two's, then three's, and forced through the streets.

"In four hours . . . (BOOM!) . . . Cservenka must be evacuated!" . . . (BOOM!) . . .

On it surged, gathering momentum as troops and refugees joined the cry, the ripple fast becoming a tidal wave threatening to drown us all.

"The Russians! . . . Run! . . . Just go! The Russians are very close!"

The noise was deafening as it crested in front of me. People were running from house to house, yelling and screaming hysterically. Already I could make out some shooting . . . heavy artillery this time . . . rumbling in the distance . . . not the rifle cracks from the hill.

I stood dumb before my window, staring almost unseeing at the madness in front of me. It was complete bedlam. The evacuation of the town was to take place along streets already filled with thousands of retreating troops, thousands of fleeing refugees . . . and a few Jews, orderly marching.

"There will no longer be time for rifle squads to continue their operation on the hill" was the only salve my imagination could find. So it had finally come. What the troops had been saying for months . . .

23

"If those rumors are true, don't wait around. Take the boys and go. Don't hesitate, because you and the children will never live. I'll never see you again." The last words of Karl as he was leaving flooded my memory.

"Mamma! What is it? What's happening?" The frightened cries of Gunther and Kurt shook me from my stupor.

"Sh-h, don't wake Norbert," I whispered hoarsely, trying to keep my panic in check. "It looks like we must leave Cservenka for a while. You must be big, brave boys now and do just as I say. We haven't much time."

Another wave of terror hit me, and I turned quickly away.

"Get hold of yourself, Kristina! Get hold . . . O God, help me. What am I going to do?"

Norbert started to whimper in his sleep, so I asked Gunther to pat him and to stay in the room until I got back. I grabbed my coat, unlocked the door, and was about to jerk it shut behind me when I saw Margaret, our maid, hurrying toward me. I had forgotten all about her.

"Oh, please, stay with the boys until I get back. Get some clothes together, some blankets, warm things, whatever you can find, and some food. I'm going to the flour mill to see about our wagon."

I was making my way through our "guests," when a couple of the soldiers yelled to me.

"See, what have we been telling you? If you want to stay alive, you have to run. Russians don't like Germans."

Pushing my way out the door into the darkness of the October night, I was met with a lightly falling drizzle. I pulled my coat collar up as tightly as I could to protect myself from the rain, and, dodging person after frantic person, I fought to keep on a straight course to the flour mill. I saw the faces of a few neighbors, some altered so much I hardly knew them as they reflected the disbelief, confusion, and the terror that gripped the heart. I knew instinctively that they were without transportation and were searching for someone, anyone, who might have room for them.

"Maybe the Russians will show some kindness to these old people," I rationalized. "After all, they are not soldiers; they are only farmers. And Yugoslavia is not at war against Russia."

I really had no idea what to expect from Russian troops. But I had seen what some Germans were doing to defenseless Jews.

"Will our fate be any better? . . .

"Officially, we are not fighting for Germany . . .

"Yet Germans occupy some of the country. . . .

"Will Russian troops distinguish between German and German?"

These ideas popped in and out of my head as I forced my way the block and a half from our house to the mill. And all the while the drums were beating, echoing what sounded like canons coming from the east. Each section of the town now had its own drummer, and the criers continued the countdown.

"Cservenka must be empty by six o'clock. It is now quarter to three. Hurry."

But they did not stop there. They had further instructions.

"Only wagons carrying German war materials will be allowed to cross the border into Hungary. Load every wagon first with German uniforms, jackets."

The night watchman was already hitching the horse to a covered wagon as I stumbled, breathless, through the doorway of the mill. Diel Baschti, a widower of about seventy with no other family, had been with the Gegners for years and years. I knew I could count on him to take charge of our wagon and to go with us as our driver.

"I'm almost ready, Frau Gegner," he called. "Try not to worry. You will be on the road before you know it."

Although I knew he was just as scared as I was, I appreciated his effort to assure me. Karl's unmarried brother, Georg, was helping as best he could, but he was very ill with tuberculosis and should have been in bed. He had been in and out of the sanatorium for years. When rumors had reached him about our immediate danger in Cservenka, he managed to get himself released and had been home for a few days. About thirty years old, he had never married because of his illness.

"How many will be in your party?" asked Diel Baschti. I did a quick calculation: Karl's sister Kati and her sixteen-year-old daughter, Martha, Georg, the three boys and I, and Diel Baschti.

"Eight," I replied, "including you."

"We will have to take both wagons."

The lead wagon, about six or seven feet long and two feet deep, had a frame we covered with a tarpaulin. Georg would have a place to lie down and both he and the food would be protected from the weather. Diel Baschti would sit in front and drive the horses. The smaller wagon, about five feet long, was linked behind and would carry military supplies which would serve as our passport into Hungary. I do not know how we did it, but within half an hour we were ready–and with yet another passenger: Kati's widowed neighbor, who sat up front with Diel Baschti and would help him with the driving.

Before we could go back to the house for the boys, however, we had to wedge our way through the unbelievable chaos in the streets to get to the center of town and the huge mountain of German military clothing. We could hardly get near the place where army personnel were heaping uniforms on wagons. Fidgety horses were neighing, and many would have broken away had there been any free space for them to move. Some people, totally out of control, continued to scream; others had calmed themselves to sobs. Children's voices (from babies' cries to youngsters' laughs and giggles) added to the din. On top of all these, domestic animals had been turned loose amid sacks and sacks of opened feed. Pigs ran wildly, squealing as they got under the hooves of horses or were nicked by the wheels of a wagon; dogs barked frantically or howled mournfully; lambs bleated; cows mooed. The scene itself was ludicrous.

Somehow we got close enough to apply for our "passport," which was immediately granted. The smaller wagon was filled level with the sides, with an extra scoop for the middle. We were also given another dose of official propaganda: "Don't worry. You will be gone from your homes only a few days. Germany will win the war."

Somehow, again, Diel Baschti got us turned around and we were headed at last along the main evacuation route which passed in front of our house. Once there, into every pocket of space we crammed the home-grown fruit, bread, salami, bratwurst, ham, and marmalade that Margaret had gotten ready, plus warm clothing, some blankets, and three pillows.

After placing Kurt and Norbert in the covered wagon with Georg and telling Gunther to climb aboard the military clothes in the back wagon, I again entered the house. I stood for a moment, alone, slowly viewing for the last time what added up to nearly ten years of life for me: the luxurious room, the thick carpets, the fine draperies, the rich oak furniture with cabinets holding crystal, silver, linen and damask. Although others would choose to deceive themselves about a soon return, I knew I would never set foot in my lovely home again. I picked up Karl's warm, leather jacket and the packet of important papers and other valuables he had set aside "just in case." On impulse, I reached for the family Bible and a photograph album. Then I turned toward the door and slowly walked outside.

I said goodbye to Margaret, who, with tears in her eyes, wished us a safe escape. She would make her way as best she could with her own people. Many, though, would be left behind as there were not enough horses. There was no way for me to contact Karl's stepmother and her daughter, Hilda; I hoped a neighbor would take care of them.

In the yard, and all around us, were more animals, running loose. I do not know what we expected would eventually become of them—a peace offering to the Russians? However, simply leaving them there to starve to death was unthinkable, even in our plight. Our pets were there: two fat little lambs, Ursula (Kurt's lamb) and Peterle (Gunther's lamb), and Hector, our beautiful dog, who sensed something was wrong. It was hard to turn our faces away.

I climbed atop the wagon, joining Gunther, Kati, and Martha. Diel Baschti called "Giddap." It was four o'clock. It was raining.

* * * * *

To make room for the hundreds of wagons now joining the train, wagons from other countries were diverted to another street so that those leaving from Cservenka could take the main road with the retreating troops. Eventually we would all merge, as farther out of town the many roads would connect with the main route. Once they began to move, wagons did not stop, not for anything except an unforeseen bottleneck which wagon masters were continually on guard to avoid. The horses would not be given a rest period either. As they walked, they would eat from gunny sacks hung around their necks. Wagons were organized into groups of twenty, with a head master over each group.

And so we left Cservenka. Everyone was crying, everyone, that is, old enough to understand what was happening. Children, including Kurt and Gunther, were excited. To them, it was high adventure. What a thrill—to get up in the middle of the night and go for a ride in a wagon, no matter the rain, howling animals, and screaming people.

As our part of the caravan moved up the street, several ran after us, begging and pleading for us to take them. But most wagons had no room. Nevertheless, some kept following, hoping to get an occasional ride for a mile or two. The train moved slowly, so it was possible for strong people to keep up on foot. But many old people without other family to care for them were left behind to take their chances with the advancing Russian Army. There were also a few who elected to stay, believing the Russians would honor a flag of surrender.

It was a sad, sad, sad night. I bundled up tightly with Gunther, and four of us sat perched atop the rough woolen uniforms . . . in the darkness . . . in the rain . . . without a cover.

"Don't cry, Mamma," he said, trying to comfort me as I drew him close. "Daddy will be back."

But I could not stop crying. I knew what those guns meant in the distance, those guns that were but a half day's march behind us. And for all I knew, Karl might have been sent to hold that front against the Russians. And now those same Russians were within ten or fifteen miles of us. And I had no idea where we were going, except that we were headed toward Hungary.

"What will we do when we get there?" I asked myself. "Go to some refugee camp? And how long will Hungary be able to hold its borders against a Russian onslaught now that Rumania has joined the Allies?"

The grey dawn did little to lift our spirits, because then the grief, although plainly audible during the night, became visible as well. It did help me some, though, to learn that another of Karl's brothers and his family were in the same group with us.

We spent the first day trying to establish a routine of how to live in an open, constantly moving wagon. It was no small chore to move the children from one wagon to another. Norbert, who was in the covered wagon with his sick uncle when we left Cservenka, soon started crying and the widow and two men were not able to care for him. Fortunately, the wagon hitch was a short one, so we could pass from one wagon to the other without sliding to the ground and running ahead. With help from Gunther, I was able to get Norbert, who needed dry diapers, on to the wagon with me. He was not happy to be changed outside in the cold. We had to hold him every second for fear he would squirm too much and fall off the wagon. Poor baby. He was hungry, too. There was no milk, so he had a sip of water and chewed on some bratwurst.

"I hope the border guards aren't too particular about what these uniforms look like after we have lived on them for a few days," I muttered.

We were only a few hours out of Cservenka and already the ride was growing tiresome for the other boys. Kurt, always active, pestered me to let him get down and run beside the wagon.

"Not yet; it's too dangerous. You might fall into some muddy ditch or get trampled by horses. You just stay put awhile," I answered. My reasons did not satisfy him completely, but he took a piece of bread, which kept him occupied for a time. Gunther was also hungry, so while Martha held Norbert, Kati and I pawed through the food and handed out pieces of bread and hunks of dried meat to everyone.

For several days before we left home, most of our meals had been eaten picnic style, but at least we had plates and cups and running water. Now we used our fingers and had only a few sips of water for drinking and nothing for washing. And at home, we had a toilet.

Ten years ago I had moved from the farm to a palace, exchanging simple manners for what was expected from one of the wealthiest ladies in the community.

"And now look at me."

"You're not sick," replied my conscience, giving me a needed stab as I though of Georg. I knew self-pity would get me little sympathy. We were all in the same miserable train. And Georg, who coughed constantly, needed good food–hot soups and lots of liquid, but nothing like that was available. He was nervous, in misery, and completely defenseless. I wondered how long he could last. Although we knew tuberculosis was highly contagious, I pushed such thoughts from my mind.

"Who cares?" I murmured to myself. "We don't know from minute to minute what will happen. We might not even make it to the Hungarian border."

We bumped along and at dusk women began to slip down from several wagons looking for an obstruction in the flat landscape which would provide some privacy for them to relieve themselves. But these were open fields with few trees, so women would hold up blankets for each other, all the while keeping an eye on their own wagons, which moved constantly ahead. Martha, Kati, the widow, and I took our turns. We soon lost our modesty.

Jani, Kati's husband, was a member of the *Volkssturm* as was Karl. Besides beautiful Martha, they had two sons. The younger one had left home some months before when, through efforts of the Red Cross, many of Yugoslavia's German children were gathered together and sent to Germany to be kept in a safe place. He was in Schleswig-Holstein, a province of Prussia near Denmark. The older son, to the dismay of his parents, had volunteered for the Nazi Youth Program in the early days of the war when several young people from Cservenka had been attracted to Hitler's movement. Martha, though, had led a very sheltered life with her parents.

As night fell, I urged Gunther to climb into the covered wagon with Kurt, and I held Norbert. I did not want him to start crawling during the night. We were heading north and slightly west toward Sombor, Yugoslavia, thirty miles away. From there it was another thirty miles to the Hungarian border. By this time, most of the troops were well ahead of us. They had trucks and could move much faster than we could. Only a few straggled behind, hurrying to catch up on foot. I was getting our morning snack assembled when I heard Norbert call.

"Look, *Mutti*! (Mamma)," he said, pointing his finger.

Two bodies lay in the roadway. I knew who they were because of the clothes they were wearing—only pajamas.

"O, dear Lord, please not here . . . not here, too!" I cried, as scenes from *Die Hohe Brücke* and from my window flashed to mind. They were lying on their faces, a dark circle in the middle of each back. I turned away, sick.

"Mamma, look! Here is another one. Mamma, look, look, look!"

But I could not look, not any longer. I cried. Later in the day, we caught up with them.

There, walking alongside the wagon train in the unpaved lane reserved for emergencies was a small band of young Jewish men. Heads bowed, faces drawn, they moved as in a trance, one foot shuffling in front of the other. They might have been some of the same ones who had passed before my eyes on the streets of Cservenka. They wore the same kinds of clothing—underwear, pajamas, blankets, some with shoes, some without. But there were not fifty in this group, only about twenty-five. The Nazi officers with them, walking or on horseback, no longer whipped them or shouted obscene commands. Instead, whenever anyone stopped or stepped out of line, he was simply shot in the back and left beside the highway. I had the feeling that some stepped out of line deliberately.

All along the train as far as I could see, no one made any move to protest what was happening to these Jews. We were, I suppose, more selfishly concerned with our own survival than in defending others, no matter how savagely they were being treated. Even on my wagon, none except the children so much as voiced their horror. Kati and Georg, like their brother Karl, seldom said much anyway. Were they now shocked speechless, or only their usual taciturn selves? And I? I thought, "It's the end anyway; there is no future for any of us." And we all turned away . . . all but the children.

Another night passed. Kati and Martha had moved to the front wagon, giving Diel Baschti and the widow a much-needed rest. Though I sensed that the shelling behind us was gradually fading, my mind was numb, dulled by the unreal all around me. There seemed to be no meaning to anything. Or perhaps my mind refused to recognize the meaning. Both the conscience and the imagination have ways of building defenses. Everything blurred–the scenery, eating, sleeping, time itself–then focused sharply every few hours as we came upon another band of Jews.

"What can we do anyway?" I continued to rationalize. "Those who had interfered back in Cservenka were shot."

We were three days into our journey to nowhere, when all of a sudden people on wagons way behind us started shouting "Gegner is coming! Gegner is coming!" It was early morning, and as the message was picked up and passed forward, the boys and I watched eagerly for our first sight of him. Everyone in Cservenka knew Gegner Karl, and as he passed wagon after wagon riding on his bicycle, cries of warm greeting were interspersed with "What's happening in Cservenka? Have the Russians taken over?" But he didn't stop until he came alongside us, hooked his bike on the back of our wagon, and climbed up on the uniforms, giving us hugs all around.

"O Karl!" I cried, clutching him. "How did you get here? I didn't think I'd ever see you again."

"When I heard Cservenka was being evacuated, I got a release to help see you safely out of Yugoslavia," he explained. "But by the time I reached home, you were already gone, so I grabbed my bicycle–

thank God it was still there—and took out after you. Are you and the boys all right?"

"Yes, but your brother is so sick I don't think he can last much longer. He coughs all the time and spits up blood."

Gunther and Kurt had not seen their father in uniform before and were fascinated with the braid, buttons, and especially his cap. Kurt begged to put it on. Gunther, more serious than his brother, looked up imploringly.

"*Vati* (Daddy), don't go away any more."

I read correctly the cloud that passed across Karl's face.

"Sh-h. Let's not talk about that right now" was all he said. He then told how frantic he had been to find us gone and our house in the possession of others. Apparently, as we moved out, many who stayed in Cservenka thought this was their chance to strike it rich. House after house was looted, including ours. Following the wave of looting, other people simply moved in. The Russian Army, he said, was involved in an effort to take Belgrade and so Cservenka had been free of military action when he passed through. Only the citizens were on the rampage, fighting among themselves like greedy heirs following the funeral.

What should have been a joyous reunion was seriously marred. I knew Karl was relieved to find us safe, but I wondered if he now knew what I had known as I left our home: there would be no going back ever to our former life. For Karl, who prided himself on being a good provider, such recognition would be devastating. I did not really know what was going through his mind, but what does it do to a man to lose his livelihood—everything he and his family have worked hard for for decades—and that in a few hours? Yet he was trying to spare me. He saw all lost, and I suffered along with him. Furthermore, Karl had never seen me dirty and disheveled; his wife was a lady. Well, there were no "ladies" left on our entire wagon train. Three days and nights lived outdoors next to the dirt is a great way to level society. In such conditions, not only is human modesty forcibly reduced, but what people are like inside quickly becomes evident, and the head masters, the only ones with weapons, took on another duty: stopping thievery. Here we were, running for our lives, seeing Jews murdered before our very eyes, and many watched for chances to steal from each other!

For a long time we bounced along in silence, keeping our

thoughts to ourselves. But then Karl never had been one to talk much. I was grateful, though, that for the time being our little family was cuddled together, even if it was on top of a wagon filled with Nazi military uniforms which we hoped would buy us safety at the Hungarian border.

* * * * *

Later, word was again passed from wagon to wagon: "We are out of the danger zone . . . we can stop."

So teach us to number our days,
That we may present to Thee a heart of wisdom. (Psalm 90:12)

Chapter Four

Reprieve and Separation

Hungary at last! I looked around apprehensively for the guards who would be inspecting our wagons. There were none. For several miles, as we rolled through the Hungarian countryside looking for a village where we might be allowed to buy milk and other supplies, I expected that we would be stopped and searched. We were not. Nobody questioned us.

"Do you suppose that was just a trick of the German military to get us to haul their gear for them?" I asked Karl. His shrug was the only answer I got. "Maybe we'll need them to enter Austria," I suggested, "but they will certainly need the cleaners by then."

We had to move a few miles inside Hungary before our group of twenty wagons could stop. With so many wagons behind us, we did not dare stop too soon and possibly cause others to be cut off on the other side of the border. Gradually, we saw signs of habitation: a small farmhouse, cultivated fields, traveled side roads indicating a village might be near. The terrain was beautiful with many evergreen trees flanking the Danube River which flowed nearby. The harvest was nearly complete, but some corn remained on the stalks. At long last, Gunther and Kurt got their chance to exercise and gladly ran into the field bordering the road, picking a few ears of corn for the horses. As we approached the village, corn fields gave way to vegetable patches of kohlrabi, carrots, and, extending into the distance, acres of sugar beets, sugar being a principal industry of southern Hungary as it was of northern Yugoslavia. I recognized also fields of wheat, rye, and oats, which had already been harvested.

Our turn to stop for rest finally came in a small village near Baja. About twenty-five modest homes made up the community of farmers. These Hungarian families were extremely hospitable and treated us very well even though they feared that a fate similar to ours might be awaiting them.

While the headmaster of our section was giving instructions for halting our wagons, several of the villagers began to gather around us, asking where we were from and the course of Russian occupation. Karl spoke Hungarian, so he had no problem understanding them, and I knew many Hungarian expressions. Because our citizenship before World War I had been with Austria-Hungary, and because of intermarriage, the German we spoke in Cservenka was mixed with Hungarian. Karl explained that the Russians had already broken into Hungary at Szeged only fifty miles due east of them and were advancing toward Budapest some hundred miles to the north.

Hungary had come to its present awkward political position through events following World War I. Under the severe terms of the Treaty of Trianon in 1920, Hungary, one of that war's losers, was stripped of two-thirds of its land, including the area where we lived. But they also lost big chunks to Rumania, Czechoslovakia, Austria, Poland, and Italy. With most of its mines and more than four-fifths of its forests gone, the nation had been near economic collapse. New industry had brought some relief, but the rise of Hitler's Germany in the 1930s proved to be a greater, if only temporary, boon.

Hoping to regain some of the lost territories, Hungarian leaders had engaged in a kind of balancing act: they did not openly support Germany, but neither did they voice vigorous opposition. And for several years the policy paid off. Ruled by a regency led by Admiral Horthy, the nation signed military agreements with Germany and profited from Hitler's early victories. First, his seizure of Czechoslovakia in 1938 brought in the Carpatho-Ukraine and part of Slovakia. Then, in 1940, it gained half of Rumania's Transylvania. Hungary, with Rumania, even joined Germany in the 1941 disastrous invasion of Russia. Yet through all this, Hungary still pinned hopes on the West, and had sent out peace feelers to the Allies, which were repeatedly ignored. So when Rumania capitulated, Hitler was understandably reluctant to leave the Eastern Front in the hands of so fickle an ally and gave Horthy an ultimatum: cooperation under German supervision or all-out occupation. Horthy chose the former, but neither nation trusted the other. Although wary of Germany, Hungarians dreaded communist Russia. Yet now, not only had this feared Russia invaded its borders, pushing its way toward the capital, but this feared Russia was now recognized by the West as an ally. Political freedom, it seemed, was being ruled out, leaving only two options: the frying pan or the fire.

Nevertheless, these particular Hungarians were not yet on the run, and they felt so sorry for us that they opened their homes and insisted we sleep in beds, if only for one night. This unexpected gesture of friendship brightened our outlook.

"Oh, if only we could take baths!" I said to Karl. "We are too dirty to sleep in someone else's bed."

First, though, as we still had provisions, we prepared our own simple meals, thus freeing our hosts from any obligation to feed us. So for the first time in many days we had a hot meal, cooked over a campfire, and with the hot food our spirits revived, and some people even told jokes. Children, of course, glad for a chance to run, were scurrying every which way, playing tag and hide-and-seek.

Before we were shown to our rooms, we were all invited to eat dessert. As we wondered what we would be served, we saw several melons, icy cold, being hauled up from the well in the yard, and we were all encouraged to gather around for a big watermelon feed. Watermelons were plentiful and easily grown in the fertile Hungarian soil, as were pumpkins—the big orange balls lay ready to harvest in nearby fields. Gunther and Kurt with several other children had a contest to see who could spit seeds the farthest. Norbert, however, simply sat and poked at the seeds with his fingers, making a big mess until I removed the seeds for him. But the frolic of the evening was soon interrupted.

The wagonmaster of our group took Karl aside to report a rumor he had heard: Karl's brother, traveling with another group of wagons from Cservenka, was missing.

"What happened?" I asked, butting in to their conversation.

"No one knows exactly," he replied. "But around midnight last night, he left the wagon to relieve himself. There was a deep, rocky ravine beside the roadway and apparently he stumbled and fell down a steep hill. He probably died right there. At least, it's better if he did," he added, "because in that pitch darkness, no one had a reasonable chance of finding him. He didn't answer when people shouted for him, and the wagons, as you know, keep right on moving. I'm sorry to bring you bad news." Karl slowly reached out to shake his hand, nodding solemnly.

"Poor Johan!" Karl sighed, quietly. "On those legs of his, he had a hard enough time to maneuver on flat ground in the daylight."

Johan, about thirty-eight years old, had been handicapped for years with *Wassersucht* (dropsy), especially in his legs, which were swollen nearly double their normal size. It was not only painful, but any moving about was difficult for him. And as the wagonmaster had reported, October nights were very dark, there being no light even from the heavens with the heavy cloud cover we had had since leaving Cservenka. I wondered what his widow would do now.

With heavy hearts, we began to clean up the rinds from the watermelons, and after visiting as best we could with our hosts, we were taken to a small bedroom reserved for guests. The family did not sleep in this room, the best one in their home. Another family would use a sofa in the living room.

In our room near one wall stood a hand-carved wooden chest covered with an embroidered white linen cloth. Placed on top was a beautifully-painted porcelain bowl with a pitcher in the middle. Clean, crisp curtains hung at the small window, and a hand-braided rug of many colors covered part of the hardwood floor. Two wall hangings, characteristic of the colorful handcrafts of many European cultures, decorated two of the walls. In the middle of the room, filling most of it, was a bed, again the best in the house. We were invited to sleep in that white, spotlessly clean, feather bed. Extra blankets were brought in for the boys and placed on the floor.

"Oh, Karl, look! We can't . . ."

"Never mind," he replied. "We must accept their hospitality. It would be worse than bad manners not to. Start to undress the boys while I fill the bowl with water from the well in the yard."

I did as he said, and he returned in a few minutes with water for washing. The boys squealed as the icy washcloths touched their bodies. Embroidered linen towels were laid out for us, and back in Cservenka, when I was a "lady," I would not have hesitated to use them. But not here; we were much too dirty. Instead, we dried ourselves with some terry towels I had brought.

Our boys settled down almost immediately. They were very tired, but also the presence of their father was always an occasion for obedient behavior. All the while gazing longingly at the white feather bed, I undressed, sponged my tired, dusty, and sweaty body, and put on the one nightgown which I found among the things Margaret had hurriedly packed. Our thoughtful hosts, realizing that Karl had nothing other than his uniform, had handed him a nightshirt when he returned with the water.

As long as I live, I don't think I will ever forget what it was to lie down in that bed. I seemed to sink down, down into whiteness, into a cloud . . . into a different world where aches, sorrow, fear cannot exist . . . into a balm, healing body and spirit alike.

"My *Kristinchen*," Karl whispered as his arms encircled me.

"O Karl," I breathed, responding to his touch and his kisses. And then, as emotional and physical exhaustion gradually overcame both of us, we slept soundly for several hours. . . . One precious night, together.

With the dawn, the anxiety which had become our constant companion returned. My cloud of healing and forgetfulness was, after all, only a feather bed, and the arms which held me would soon be holding something cold and metallic. Karl and I dressed quietly, but not quietly enough for Norbert. He sat upright on his blanket and grinned.

"*Mutti!* (Mamma!)." He looked around the room, his grin replaced by a quizzical expression, as if he were asking "Where am I?" His call aroused Kurt and Gunther and my one precious night had ended indeed.

Karl was not used to helping me with the children, but there were no servants here. So he coaxed the older boys to dress themselves while I tended to Norbert. The smell of coffee permeated the room and my mouth began to water. We were not going to leave with empty stomachs. First, though, we all marched out to the yard and washed our hands and faces with water from a trough.

Within a few minutes, all who had slept under that roof that night were standing together around a table spread with homemade bread (which had been baked in a mud oven outdoors) and butter, dried, smoked sausage, milk, and coffee mixed with chicory. All served themselves, then went outside into the yard, for the room was very crowded. At first, people greeted one another warmly, the rest of the previous night being reflected in happy voices. But little by little, as we anticipated the sad farewells and the uncertain future, the tones grew somber. While we finished eating, our wagonmaster arranged to buy as much food as the farmers could spare and paid cash for it.

After the men and boys loaded the wagons and tended to the horses, the women gathered the children and prepared to climb aboard the wagons. Villagers once again encircled us, shaking our hands and hugging us, many with tears in their eyes, many with folded hands as if praying. The women, all of them, wore dark clothes with scarves tied under their chins. Some had on the plain Hungarian *Drachten* (costume) made up of three dirndl skirts on top of each other. In these black skirts and dark blue blouses and with black scarves tied around their heads, they all looked eighty years old. Their dress intensified the grave atmosphere. Gone was the hilarious spirit of earlier years when these people tried to outdo one another with colors and beauty. I remembered having seen such carefree and gentle Hungarians, both men and women, on the way to church, all dressed up in their bright colors—greens, reds, blues. The usually big-busted women had worn tight-fitting, glistening white blouses and caps on their heads; men, too, wore white shirts (though loose-fitting) and bright caps. Not so on this day: there were no bright colors; there was no rejoicing.

Aboard the wagons once again, we slowly formed a line behind our wagonmaster. As our wagon began to roll, we waved reluctantly to the Hungarian families who had showed us so much kindness. Some walked alongside, giving a few last words of encouragement. Although the Red Army was only a few miles east of us, we heard no shooting from that direction. "I hope our paths don't cross," I said to myself.

Watered, fed and rested, our horses pulled with renewed energy. To relieve Diel Baschti, Karl would drive our wagon as we continued to move deeper into Hungary on our way to Vienna. Maybe we would be safe there. I joined Karl on the seat of the front wagon and held on to little Norbert. Georg, still coughing and very weak despite the hot food, was returned to his bed in the covered part of the lead wagon, and Kurt and Gunther squeezed in beside him and next to the parcels of food. The others—the widow, Kati, Martha, and Diel Baschti—rode in the cart with the uniforms. After a few groups of twenty wagons had passed us, we got our turn to join up with the main body of the train. Because bridges were being blown up, the decision was made to cross the Danube River while we had the chance at the bridge at Baja, then aim for Dunaföldvár and skirt large Lake Balaton at its northern end.

As far as we could see were wagons, wagons, and more wagons: a scene of confusion, but not the frenzy of our departure from Cservenka. And we could be thankful, after all, that it was not wintertime. The air was chilly, but harsh weather was not yet upon us, and the rain had stopped. And I had my husband with me, and I wanted to keep him.

"I'll drive for a few hours," he promised. "I want to make certain of your place in the wagon train and get some idea of the route you'll be taking before I leave." But I begged him to stay with us.

"With everything falling apart," I pleaded, "who will know or care where you are? Anyway, what's more important than our being together and trying to stay alive?" Karl did not answer. He only looked at me strangely, and I could not read his thoughts.

I cuddled Norbert closer and buried my face in his blanket, trying to console myself. How little I really knew the man I had lived with for almost ten years. Oh, I knew where he had gone to school, that he had traveled extensively all over the world and had spent several years in the United States, and that he, along with all our neighbors of German ancestry, was totally opposed to Communism. Also, as was the case with other Yugoslav Germans, he resented that we were considered second-class citizens. In Germany, people had more freedom than we had. However, I was uncertain of his full views about this war. His caring for me had centered mainly on the material comforts of life. Whether he thought me incapable of philosophical discussions, I was not sure. But we never had them.

I stole a glance at Karl, who, from his sober staring into space, seemed absorbed in thought. Again lowering my head, I tried to imagine what Karl was thinking about our future. If the alternative turns out to be Communism under Tito or possibly under Russia, is not a victory for Germany our only hope? After all, our language and cultural patterns are German and we never have had much in common with our Serbian neighbors. On the other hand, what kind of victors would they be? What values do we have in common with the beastiality I had seen? Any momentary glimmer of hope I had felt was abruptly erased by *Die Hohe Brücke* . . . pistol shots . . . the snapping of whips, the screams, the obscene shouts, the barefoot figures in pajamas or blankets . . . . I shook myself, both physically and mentally.

"I'll stay with the train for one day." Karl spoke deliberately while reaching for my hand. "Then I must go; I must." From his tone I knew it was futile to say anything more. Was it a sense of duty that drove this man? Duty toward Yugoslavia? But Yugoslavia had no army and Karl was not part of the Chetniks. Duty toward the Germans who administered part of Yugoslavia? It was all so unclear–politics, duty, even right and wrong seemed hopelessly muddled. The only thing that was clear was my frustration about our being parted again and having to go on alone with our boys to Vienna. And then what?

Vienna was only a part of what was becoming for me a no-man's land. I was on my way into nowhere and would not return this way. Somehow I knew that Cservenka was forever lost to me. Yet I did not then grasp the extent of my actual "nowhere." I had lost my beautiful home and my possessions, and the sting of those losses I would feel for years to come. Also lost to me at that time was my real poverty–my poverty of spirit. Although my passing into nowhere would at last lead to somewhere, infinitely more important, it would lead to Someone.

However, lying now only a few miles ahead of me was physical devastation, the rubble caused by the machinery of war. So far I had not seen the battle, but I had seen the chaos brought about by the threat of destruction. Even more disturbing, I had caught sight of the minds behind the machinery–minds exposed through their ruthless, fanatical brutality against Jewish people. The full weight of that horror would not be mine to carry, and, compared to that, what I would bear is unequal in comparison. But on 11 October 1944, as I rode uncomfortably into the heart of Hungary in a covered wagon with only separation from my husband to look forward to, my frustration had already given way to self-pity, then anger. Yet I suffered in silence.

On we rolled. The boys were increasingly restless and Kurt and Gunther kept asking where we were going and where we would live when we got there. They were too young to be fully sensitive to what was happening, and I was thankful for that. The squirmer Norbert, of course, needed constant attention. I was getting completely worn out trying to keep him fed, changed, and entertained. Also, getting lost was always a danger whenever anyone jumped from the wagons to "go to the bathroom." Therefore, being forced to keep an alert eye on the children, as the day wore on I was unable to nurse my self-pity.

Autumn days were growing shorter and as the sun lowered, so did the temperature. Shivering myself, I urged everyone to bundle up and reminded them that we would soon be taking turns trying to sleep while the wagons kept rolling.

I dreaded the night because I knew it would be my last one with Karl. And this night would not be spent in a clean, feather bed. There would be no consoling arms, no words of comfort. In fact, there would be no real sleep either–and not only because it was nearly impossible to get into a comfortable position on top of the military uniforms which would be our bed in the back wagon.

To change positions on moving carts is almost as precarious as moving about in a row boat. However, we all made the transfer, Diel Baschti once more taking the reins so Karl could rest before leaving at dawn. We ate some bread, cheese, and a few mouthfuls of the milk we had bought that morning. As I set aside some food for Karl to take with him, I longed for a cup of hot coffee to stop my shivering. My shivering, though, was not caused solely by the chilly air.

Gradually, the horizon drew closer as night tightened around us. By rearranging a few uniforms, Gunther and Kurt had managed to hollow out a place big enough for the two of them where they cuddled together to gain warmth from each other. Karl and I, taking turns holding Norbert, were finding it hard to get comfortable when we caught sight of a wagonmaster, who was riding alongside the train two wagons back of us. He usually made the rounds on horseback, checking on the wagons under his charge and passing along any news he might have heard from people in our group or from other wagonmasters. The grapevine was fairly effective. This time, however, hearing the groans that came in reply to whatever it was he said, I felt the muscles in my stomach and throat tighten.

"Now what?" I said, directing my harsh whisper to Karl. Because of the noise of the wheels, we were unable to overhear everything he said to those on the wagon directly behind us, but we did catch the warning "Watch your children!" and soon learned the reason for his stern command.

"A baby fell from its mother's lap and has been crushed beneath the wheels," he told us. Apparently, as she dozed off and her grip relaxed, the infant had slipped from her protective arms, and for several minutes she had not realized what had happened. "The mother," he continued, "is almost insane." As we would learn later, there had been other such incidents at night. Yet the wagons kept going, carrying guilt-stricken, grieving mothers whose babies were not seen again unless by someone following after who might bury a little blanket with its pitiful remains.

Sickened, I grabbed a sleeping Norbert with such fierceness that he woke up. His cry, which usually upset me, this time was music: he was alive.

As the miles dragged by, anxious and cold as I was, I still did not wish for time to pass more quickly. The new day would usher in another kind of night and the emotional darkness I anticipated without Karl was worse than nature's night. I clung to Norbert and, in spite of myself, dozed occasionally. I don't remember if I dreamed in sleep, but whenever I would awaken, the nightmarish daydream of recent days continued, scene after scene toppling nilly-willy into my mind. Nevertheless my dread of the new day had no effect on time, which pushed steadily forward to meet it and revealed the grey, pre-dawn sky.

Karl called to Diel Baschti, asking him to pull out of the train for a minute so he could untie his bike. Perhaps sensing something was wrong, Norbert grabbed for his *Vati's* leg, as if trying to hold on to him. His action was the most emotional of our goodbye. Karl reached for each of us for a last hug and kiss, telling Gunther and Kurt, "Obey your mother and be good." I murmured a silly "We are going to win the war." Karl said nothing in reply, only stuffed the bread and cheese into his military knapsack, jumped from the wagon, and loosened his bike. While Diel Baschti pulled our wagon into line once again, Karl mounted his bicycle and, turning around very quickly, called, "Back to my company." That was all he said. I did not question; I did not cry. I simply watched his figure blend into the grey landscape, totally ignorant of the threat young Kurt had overheard at the time Karl left in September—a threat Karl never told me about: "Take your choice: either fight for Germany . . . or be shot."

Seek the LORD while He may be found;
Call upon Him while He is near. (Isaiah 55:6)

Chapter Five

An Unexpected Reunion

October 13, 1944. How fateful the next few days were to be in the see-sawing battle for Budapest. With Soviet troops already far inside Hungary, German troops and their Hungarian allies together with refugees were retreating from east Hungary. The week ahead would register heavy bombing of the capital by the Allies, revolt against Germany by Hungarian leaders in the city, and retaliation by Hitler. All the while, only a few miles east of us, another part of the Red Army would continue its advance on Budapest from the south. The ominous events of these days history has recorded. We on the wagon train, however, were unaware of what was happening, yet we would cross a line of fire.

After Karl left, the rest of us observed the usual routine of a new day. We first took turns getting off the wagons, taking advantage of the screen the semi-darkness provided. Then we brought out the bread and Martha distributed a hunk to each of us, except Georg. The poor man was growing weaker by the hour, but there was nothing we could do to help him. He took only a few sips of liquid. Although the dry bread was cotton in my mouth, I mechanically went through the motions of chewing. My husband's leaving was like a death in the family, and I had no appetite. That I had three small boys to watch out for was the discipline that kept me going for the next few hours. I felt so completely helpless and depressed that I might have given in to despondency were it not for them. Kurt and Gunther piled up question upon question and I tried to come up with reassuring answers to their barrage.

"Mamma, where is Daddy going?"

"I'm not sure, Kurt." Mustering a weak smile, I turned to look at him and Gunther. "But wherever it is, he will help the war get over sooner." I tried to keep my voice steady, but as I began to review the information I did have, I saw a shrinking of safe territory as Nazi forces steadily withdrew from previously conquered lands. Border countries were falling to the Russians; Italy had changed sides; the Allies were in France and Italy. Karl must be with the Germans. It did not make sense otherwise.

"Mamma, when is Daddy coming back to ride with us?"

"I don't really know that either, Gunther. Maybe he'll be waiting for us when we get to Vienna." Wishful thinking indeed!

"Mamma, is Daddy going to shoot people?"

Stunned by such words coming from the mouth of a six-year-old, I struggled to retain an outward composure. Killing had become all too real, even for children. During the last few days, they had already seen triggers pulled, heard the sharp cracks, and watched the targeted men fall to the ground. What could I say? Soldiers carry guns and shoot them. Children in their "pretend" games have some knowledge of warfare, but in a game those who are "shot" always get up and change sides with their "enemy." They repeat the process until they get bored, at which time the war ends happily and everyone goes home unhurt. Gunther and Kurt had now seen that people who are shot with real guns bleed real blood. Furthermore, they do not get up again. My hesitation must have prompted the follow-up questions.

"Mamma, is anyone going to shoot Daddy? Is he going to be killed?"

I felt the color drain from my cheeks. Only words, tumbling innocently from my young son's mouth, yet they left me limp. Gunther must have noticed the change in me, for his face, which had shown only a quizzical curiosity, suddenly sobered. Kurt, on the other hand, fired both barrels again.

"Is Daddy going to shoot anyone? Is Daddy going to be killed?" This time, though, my response was quite different.

"Of course not! No, of course not!" I replied with cocky confidence. "Daddy is going to help people . . . people like us who have to leave their homes for a little while until the war is all over."

Satisfied with this answer, they switched their attention and started poking each other in the manner of playful brothers. It was not that simple for me. I was alone again and would have to face whatever lay ahead. Dreaded possibilities had now been given a reality in words. Pretending might shield me for a time, but sooner or later . . .

Would I be ready? I wondered. Giving words to my fears had one advantage: I could sift some possibilities and come to terms with each beforehand. This war had already made hundreds of thousands of widows. "And maybe," I thought, giving in to childish fancy, "putting the worst into words will guarantee it won't happen—or is it the other way around?"

After a few minutes of this unhealthy mode of thought, I hauled myself up and volunteered to drive the wagons. Diel Baschti thanked me for my offer and was slowing the horses so we could change places, when we heard the airplanes. For days we had been aware of the distant rumble of high-flying aircraft, but this was different.

We searched the sky where the noise was coming from. Planes on the horizon approached rapidly and were soon upon us. To our great relief, the squadron streaked over us without incident. But then . . .

"Who in the world would mow down refugees?" yelled Diel Baschti, when to our amazement the next group began firing on our caravan. "Quick! everyone off the top where you are sitting ducks and get under the wagon! I'll pull out of line."

I grabbed Norbert and followed Gunther and Kurt, who had already slid to the ground. As soon as the horses were stopped, I pushed the boys to the earth, shoved them under the cart, and wriggled under myself. Only Georg remained on the wagon, under a cover which would give little protection should a bullet strike there.

Like fire, panic spread among the wagons, creating a scene similar to the one on evacuation day in Cservenka. Some horses bolted with wagon and all in response to the screaming people and the artillery from the planes overhead, leaving their owners stranded in the open. Many shots hit the surrounding dirt, spraying mud into the air; some hit pavement, ricocheting here and there; others struck the wooden wagons; and a few found their way into human flesh. The actual attack lasted only a minute or two, but as the planes continued on their mission, the confusion left in their wake continued for hours.

It was nightfall before all the wagons in our vicinity were under control. Yet the apparent order did not give an accurate picture of the inner chaos which had gripped the train. Before we had reached Hungary, we had been terrified of the troops who pursued us on the ground. However, we believed we had a chance to outrun them. But what protection did we have from air assault? We were visible for miles in every direction—a long snake winding its way into the heart of Hungary. For some, the strain had proved too much, and suicides began to be reported among us.

Because we had lost valuable time and had not made as much progress as usual, our wagonmaster urged us to keep up a slow pace during the night. "After we get closer to Austria," he said, "we will stop each night."

We tried. For a few hours we kept pace. But when the wagonmaster of our group made his regular evening rounds, he began advising each driver to watch for the cue to form two circles. We would stop for the night after all. It seems he had conferred with other wagon masters and they had agreed it would be better to stop. We had no young men with us, and the older men and women who were doing the driving were dangerously weary in addition to being frightened by the shooting, which had taken some lives.

"The darkness will protect us from any night raids," I heard him tell Diel Bashti, "and you folks can try for a little sleep in peace. No one knows what's in store for tomorrow," he confessed. "I want everyone as quick-witted as possible then." He rode to the front wagon and started to lead the way for the first group of ten to follow and repeated the process for us in the second batch. It was a relief to stop the bouncing, and as soon as the circle was formed, we gratefully jumped down and got some much-needed exercise. I was glad, too, to be free of all the worries associated with travel at night. The picture of a baby beneath moving wheels was still fresh in my mind. The stopping also gave people a chance to exchange news from other parts of the train, which this time brought me another sadness but a bright ray, too.

In the first case, we learned that the tiny infant of Karl's cousin had died. The turmoil of our escape from Cservenka had caused the milk of the nursing mother to dry up and she did not have bottles or safe-to-drink fresh milk for a baby only a few weeks old. I grieved for her, but felt a surge of hope from what I heard next: my sister Sophia was in a group of wagons now only a short distance behind and her husband, Josef, was hurrying as fast as he could to catch us. They lived near the Senta River of the Banat region a few miles south and west of Szeged, where the Red Army had entered Hungary.

The prospect of seeing my sister greatly revived my spirits. I felt a little guilty, too. Having been so wrapped up in my own problems, I had not thought much at all about the fate of members of my family who lived in other parts of Yugoslavia. At last I would have someone of my own flesh and blood to commiserate with. Not only that, I hoped against hope that she would have room for the boys and me. With Georg so sick and requiring the covered wagon, it meant that the rest of us were almost always outside on top of German uniforms.

Actually, having the uniforms was proving to be a blessing: they made great "tents." Under them, Kurt and Gunther would giggle with delight, and they also furnished some protection from the cold and rain. As soon as they became soaked through, we got rid of the soggy things by tossing them out beside the roadway. In this manner, we gradually lightened the load and found extra space for ourselves, too.

Each day, though, brought another layer of dirt and more smells, which had their effect on our manners. It was bad enough for us who could manage a minimum of personal hygiene with the little water we reserved for washing whenever we came upon a creek, small stream, or a pond. It became increasingly difficult to care for Georg, however. And poor little Norbert! I had long since exhausted his diaper supply and I could not wash the dirty ones. We were cold, we were tired, we were dirty.

Sophia was the sister who had gone to the United States, then returned a few years later to get married. She and Josef had one daughter, Ibi, about ten years old, and they were well off because Josef made a good living as a wine distributor. I wondered about the story they had to tell. "Did they," I asked myself, "have to leave everything on a moment's notice?" Tired as I was, it was hard for me to get any sleep as the night wore steadily on.

It was still dark when the wagonmaster summoned the twenty drivers under his supervision to meet with him for instructions regarding the day's schedule. He wanted every driver to have a plan for protection in case planes would fire on us again. Once that was determined, we all ate from our diminishing storehouse and began once more to form a line. I was reluctant to move; I did not want to put further distance between my sister and me. Others were sympathetic and agreed to let us stay put and join the train with another group later. We were still discussing the matter when someone in the Cservenka section started shouting, "Wait! Frau Gegner's sister is coming! Wait!"

"O Sophia!" I cried, as I ran toward the quick-moving wagon approaching through the misty atmosphere. "Sophia!"

"Kristina! Is that really you?" she called back as she climbed down from the wagon. "I didn't think we'd ever catch up with you." We fell on each other, crying and laughing hysterically. "Everything is going to be all right," she said between sobs. "When this is over, we can go back to our homes."

"Of course we will; of course, we'll go back!" I agreed, crying and hugging her fiercely. I knew better. "But how did you find me? How is it that Josef is with you? Why isn't he fighting like everybody else? Karl had to go. Why doesn't Josef? Why . . ."

"Slow down, Kristina, please. One question at a time. Many who heard of Karl's visit knew you were in the train somewhere ahead of us. The Gegner name is well-known in the Batschka, you know, so we decided to pull out of line and try to catch up with you ourselves. We just kept asking questions. We asked about Anna, too, but no one knew her whereabouts. Have you seen her?"

"No," I admitted. "But the confusion in Cservenka the day we left was awful. She's probably with her husband's people, and probably up ahead, since you didn't pass her," I guessed. Anna's husband would not be fighting, I was certain, because of disabling injuries he had received in World War I. Our other sister, Kati, was a widow; her husband's family would look after her. As for our brothers still living, Josef was a member of the *Volkssturm* in Slovenia, so he, like my Karl, was probably separated from his family. Georg, the oldest surviving, had returned to Cservenka from New York to take over the farm when our father died. He had a severe limp from a foot injury he received when a boy, so he was unfit for military duty. And Peter—Sophia and I were both thankful that he had stayed in the United States and that he was too old to be drafted.

"Hurry!" Sophia urged. "We can get caught up on the way. Get your things together. You and the boys are coming with us."

I did not need to be coaxed. Ibi had already greeted her cousins and Josef was helping the children into the wagon while I gathered up my portion of the remaining food and our other belongings, giving special attention to the small suitcase which held the Bible, picture album, and important papers. Most of the clothes were already on our backs. I hugged each and said goodbye to Georg. I believed we were saying goodbye forever. Yet despite the seeming finality of our parting, I thought it was welcomed by them as much as it was by me. On impulse, I offered them two of my three pillows. I felt bad that they would still have to ride without a cover, but they would be less crowded. My children would now be better protected from the weather and have space to sleep comfortably once in a while.

Sophia's wagon was like a house trailer. Covered with canvas, it had fiberglass windows, and its cozy little room was the size of our two wagons put together. And there were no uniforms! In that setting, it seemed like heaven. The bed with its red coverlet was rolled up during the day to allow added floor space. Sophia carried water in five-gallon jugs and had plenty of washcloths, so we were able to keep our hands and faces clean. Also, they came away with far more clothes than the boys and I had. Sophia and Josef must have given their packing some careful thought, because everything was well-organized—what a contrast to the last-minute grabbing I had done.

"We knew it would only be a matter of time unless that new weapon we kept hearing about was used very soon," she explained. "So we had been ready for a quick get-away for over two weeks." I wished I had been more serious about the warnings.

As we started to move, the drizzle continued, but this time I did not mind. I was inside and I had a bench to sit on. I also had a cup of hot coffee to drink. Yes, Sophia was prepared; she had even brought along a small kerosene stove and fired it up just so I could have a cup of coffee. Perhaps the worst of my journey to nowhere was over; perhaps there was reason to hope after all.

My optimism increased when later that day planes again zoomed overhead and not one of them fired at us. Josef's opinion was that the shooting of the day before resulted from a mistake in judgment—that the pilots of fighter planes must make snap decisions because the planes move at high speeds. "It might have been deliberate harassment, but it might also have been a case of 'shoot first and ask questions later'—from the air we might look like a military column," he said, adding that it probably meant also that bombers were flying high above them.

Our fortune indeed seemed to change for the better as we

progressed toward the Austrian border. We went faster than most due to good horses and the modern trailer. When we came near villages, some Hungarians came out to the road to watch us, several of them with food to sell. The caravan was now segmented, as group after group decided on its own destination. We kept well west of Budapest as we moved northward, and after leaving the vicinity of Székesfehérvár, several headed straight for the Czechoslovakian border. Others of us aimed toward Györ and Vienna.

Unknown to us, meanwhile, was the drama in Budapest. The capital was the target of heavy bombing by Allied forces,[2] probably Americans based in southeast Italy. It is reasonable to suppose those were the very planes that flew over us. With Allies pounding the Nazis as far east as the Hungarian capital, Admiral Horthy tested Hitler's yoke and told the Hungarian nation that he was about to sign an armistice with the Allies. He was immediately checked: by kidnapping his son and threatening his execution, the Nazis forced a broken Horthy to recant and abdicate. The date was 15 October 1944.

The total collapse of Horthy's government seemed to doom completely the attempts to save what was left of European Jews who had sought that city as a refuge. All through the spring and summer of 1944, after Horthy submitted to Hitler's ultimatum and chose to accept German supervision in order to hold back total occupation by German forces, the Nazi dragnet, with fewer and fewer loopholes, had tightened around the entrapped Jews. And despite frantic efforts, which continued in the face of a Nazi holdout that was to last four months, when Russians "liberated" the city on 13 February 1945, only about 120,000 of the Jews cornered in the city during 1944 remained. Hundreds of thousands died.[3]

Among us, however, except for telling how we left home, there was not much discussion about the war. We were occupied mainly with caring for the children. At first I was very happy about having the company of my sister and the better conditions for travel. After a couple of days, though, I felt like an intruder in their personal lives. Sophia and Josef no longer had any privacy, and the surroundings were so cramped for seven people that we seldom slept all at once. Next, I began to grow jealous of Sophia because she had a husband and I did not. I sensed also their reluctance to answer my questions about why Josef was not fighting. I was able to indulge myself in what now seems petty only because the time and the miles were passing without serious incident.

* * * * *

About ten miles from the Austrian border, we passed through what became for me an incongruous interlude. It was early in the morning, and, for a change, it was not raining, when we came upon a small Armenian village. Pulling aside to rest and see if we could buy food, we stopped near one of the farmhouses and Gunther, Kurt, and Ibi jumped from the wagon and had a race to a close-by tree. I helped Norbert to get down and he toddled after them. Soon three women, perhaps a mother and two teenage daughters, all wearing long, dark skirts and ruffled bonnets and carrying milk buckets, emerged from a red barn and walked toward us, smiling warmly. Like something from another century, they reminded me of pictures I had seen of the early Pilgrims in America.

Extending her hand, the mother welcomed us in a dialect of a hundred years back that sounded like Dutch. We had to listen very intently to understand what she was saying, but we were able to make out her offer of fresh milk and bread. We nodded our acceptance and she beckoned us to follow. After gathering the children and washing our hands and faces, we entered a clean, bright kitchen that was as primitive as the people themselves: the furnishings were handmade and there were no modern appliances, not even electricity. I noticed a big tub with a washboard and a hand-operated churn. With no machinery of any kind, even their plowing continued in the fashion of a by-gone century.

We gratefully ate the freshly-baked dark bread which she set before us on the handwoven cloth covering the table. The milk we drank was still warm, having recently come from the cow. I felt strangely at home. All was good and unspoiled, bringing to mind my very early years on the farm outside Cservenka. But more than that. These folk had a pure contentment, a calmness of spirit which transformed the humble, earthly setting into something beautifully otherworldly. They obviously belonged to another time; they seemed also to belong to another world. Here, I sensed, was true peace, and something deep inside me did not want to leave.

As we finished eating, we were joined by the woman's husband, who had completed his morning chores and was intending to have his breakfast. But first, motioning for Josef to follow, he showed him where to feed and water the horses, and all too soon we were on our way again.

The interlude had ended, and although the hardship of the road soon returned, my sense of well-being remained. The closer we came to Austria, the more excited we grew. To be with our German-speaking brothers and sisters—for that is what we considered them to be—was all we could think of and talk about. We anticipated a reception similar to the one in the Armenian village. Why we expected to be welcomed with open arms, I don't know; but that is fully what we expected. Instead, ahead lay bitter disappointment of which Vienna, Strauss's "city of dreams," would be only the beginning.

Make me know Thy ways, O LORD,
Teach me Thy paths. (Psalm 25:4)

Chapter Six

Vienna: A Safe Place?

Tired as we were, our feelings of elation became both our buoy and spur. We were entering country new to me and I was eager to see the glories associated with Vienna, a city so rich in history and the arts. Despite all the mixed-up ideas I had about the war in terms of allegiance, and despite my morbid certainty that I never would return to live again in Cservenka, I still harbored deep within me the belief that if I could only reach the true German stock from which I had come, then I would be safe. Those Germans were hard workers with close family ties, friendly, outgoing, warm, not at all like the Nazis I had seen. I also hung on to the hope that further inland lay security. Even though all the nations surrounding Germany should collapse, the inner core would surely be safe, whichever way the war finally went. In this manner, I nursed my hope.

The children, too, must have caught our spirit of optimism, for while Norbert napped, the others questioned where we would stay in Vienna. They had not seen a big city before and their eyes widened to our reports of things they might see there. I had not seen a city other than Belgrade either, so I could not speak from personal experience, only from what I had read and from what I remembered Karl had told me. At my mention of Karl, Gunther and Kurt immediately started asking about their father, rekindling anew my emotional panic and disrupting the inner calm I was experiencing since our visit to the Armenian village. I side-stepped their questions and tried to interest them in one of the games Sophia had had the foresight to bring. How grateful I was when they were soon involved in a card game.

One indication that we were getting nearer to Austria was the traffic. We had gotten well ahead of our groups from the Banat and the Batschka because of Josef's fast wagon. Here, we were rolling into an earlier wave. The closer we came to the border, the worse it became, until we were once again bunched together, then stopped. Inching our way, we came eventually to Hegyeshalom and the boundary, and, as had been the case when we entered Hungary, the border was completely unguarded, as if no one cared who came or went.

"Well, it appears we really did carry a lot of German uniforms for nothing," I remarked while viewing the jammed intersection into which we had moved. Josef had simply ignored a similar order in his home town.

"I never did believe that story about border checks," he had said when we recounted our getaways earlier. "And anyway, with all the confusion it would be impossible to check everyone, and besides," he added, "the German military has more urgent problems than keeping tabs on some uniforms."

How right he was. Were there other orders he had ignored, too, I wondered, such as reporting for duty? I felt myself slipping into resentment again. Josef had always been cunning, always one who figured the odds, which probably counted toward his success in the business world. Karl, on the other hand, played by the rules and obeyed, usually without question, whatever an authority required of him. I had admired the trait in Karl, but in this case I kept asking myself what was to be gained by serving a losing cause–and at the very last moment. Also, although we had not come across more groups of Jews, I could not forget what I had seen, nor could I forget that it was done by Germans. In this way, my hope was constantly buffeted by my misgivings.

But we were in Austria; we had gotten this far, and safely. And already Josef and Sophia were talking about their expected return to the Banat.

"You saw through the empty threat of carting military uniforms, but still you believe the propaganda about returning to our homes right away?" I asked, incredulously. Surely the shrewd Josef could not be taken in by promises of a soon return. Even I knew better than that, and I had gotten the impression that Karl knew it too. Yet all the way to the outskirts of Vienna, which took a whole day and night with no stops, Sophia and Josef talked of little else. They actually hoped to be home by Christmas.

By this time, carts and wagons were all over the street and the noise was terrible. We could hardly move. Gradually we began to take note of carts and wagons, hundreds of them, left in the grassy places alongside the roadway, and the closer we got to the city, the more abandoned wagons we saw.

"I wonder what this means," Sophia and I said, almost at the same time. We had reached our first checkpoint.

No wagons or horses were being allowed in the city, we discovered, and we were soon met by German officers on horseback ordering us to find a place off the roadway and to take with us only what we could carry. Carry? Yes, we would make our way from here on foot. Josef was angry, but he had no choice but to follow these orders. Furthermore, we could see ahead that there was a barricade blocking the way for all vehicles.

"And what about my horses?" he yelled after the officers.

"You'll leave them, too," one shouted back. "But don't worry," added another. "We'll give you a receipt."

A receipt? I could have howled with laughter. The place was bedlam—for miles around, the carts and wagons were becoming more tightly packed by the minute. The horses, though tired, were not indifferent to the impatient, short-tempered humans swarming around them, and their bucking and trampling scared many. There was about as much order as one would find in a barnyard fire. A receipt!

"Can't we sleep on the wagon tonight and start walking tomorrow morning when it gets light?" I asked. It was dangerous to get off the wagon, and it was already dark. I got my answer from a barked command: "Everyone to the camp now . . . as soon as possible!"

And so we packed for our move. I bundled up three very tired boys and put on Karl's leather jacket. I handed a food satchel to Kurt, the small suitcase which held a few articles of clothing plus the Bible, photograph album, and valuables to Gunther, and picked up the pillow and Norbert. Sophia gathered together as much as the three of them could carry, and we were off for our night on the town. It was cold and we could hardly see where we were going, because the streets were dark. All lights had been turned off to make night bombing more difficult. At the barricade, Josef stopped for his receipt—he really did get one—and to talk things over with the officers.

The rest of us slowly made our way, joining the throngs shuffling along the crowded sidewalks. Mounted Austrian police shouted directions.

When Josef caught up with us, he said refugees were being housed in a big building near the famous Vienna Opera House. That sounded encouraging; at least we would be in a good section of the city.

"Maybe the big building is a hotel," I said, conjuring up in my mind a vision of a clean, heated room with a feather bed, sheets and blankets, and a bathtub.

"Well, if it is a hotel, we won't be put up in style," Josef chided. "Look at all these people!" There were thousands of us on the streets that night. As I could not hold Norbert much longer and he was too tired to walk, I was grateful to Josef when he offered to carry him. We exchanged loads.

After a mile or so, we came to our second checkpoint. It was not a hotel. In the darkness it looked rather like a gymnasium surrounded by a park-like area. We joined the lines and lines of people pushing their way to get inside to the desk, where we would be issued a name card with an identification number. With that transaction, we became subject to the regulations pertaining to refugees and were eligible for food and medical care.

While we were still in the street awaiting our turn to be assigned, Josef spied someone from the Banat whom he knew. I do not know what they talked about, but he conferred right away with Sophia, and afterwards they both told me that they would keep moving, as this camp was for women and children only. However, because they thought I would be quite safe here in Vienna, they had decided to leave Ibi with me and the boys.

I was dumbfounded. But that is exactly what my sister and her husband did. As soon as they knew there was room for us in downtown Vienna, they hugged us all. "We'll be back to pick up Ibi and then we'll all go home," Josef assured me. And with that they left with the friend from the Banat. I suppose they thought a young girl would be safer in a supervised refugee camp than with them on the road somewhere, in case they encountered Russian military, yet I considered the added responsibility to be an unfair burden. Ibi was a good girl and would not deliberately cause trouble, but she was another human that I would have to watch out for and a child at that.

For the first time since leaving Cservenka, I had only children for companions. I had no idea where Karl's family was. Although I believed I had made the right choice when I agreed to leave their company in favor of my sister's, fear started welling up. I really was on my own.

We stood near a big desk in the entryway and stared into the adjoining huge room. There were no beds, not even mattresses, only straw such as one finds in animal stalls. A woman guard spoke gruffly to me, breaking into my trance, and I and the children followed her to the section allotted to us and sat down with our belongings on the straw. Our area was about six feet square.

"There are public toilets and wash basins down the corridor where you came in," she said, walking away. So we got in line again and waited our turn.

About two thousand people slept on that floor that night. I was thankful for my pillow and two blankets, and we bedded right down and fell asleep almost immediately. We were exhausted. With morning came the realization that not everyone had slept during the night. The small suitcase containing my few treasures was missing; so was the pillow.

The family Bible listed names of people who spanned some two hundred years of the Gegner family history. The pictures also could never be replaced. Fortunately, I had taken some of them from the album and had placed them in my purse, and I was wearing the few pieces of gold jewelry. All the legal papers, however, were gone. And the pillow–the boys must have rolled off it, or else someone actually took it from under their heads. If any had witnessed the robbery, they did not speak up, and I knew it was futile to report the incident. I felt heartsick and also exposed and humiliated, knowing that someone had very personal information about me and my family and I did not know who it was.

Dawn also brought unbelievable confusion as two thousand women and children bestirred themselves for a new day. There were young women with infants and toddlers, women with primary age children, grandmothers with or without children. Many were apprehensive at having been separated from a mate or older son; all were homeless in a country not their own; many were crying; many looked disoriented and hopeless; all were dirty and unkempt; most were stiff from sleeping on the floor; everyone was hungry; everyone had to use the bathroom.

After we shoved and fought our way through the bathroom and into the line for breakfast, we were handed banged-up metal cups and served hot oatmeal and black bread. Only the very young children got milk to drink; the rest of us had brewed chicory with saccharin (no sugar) for a sweetener. Norbert qualified for milk, but not the other three, who looked longingly at the jug of white liquid.

Back on our straw pad and eating our rations, I suddenly got the idea to try to contact the family of the Austrian boy who had stayed with us for several months during the spring and summer. "If I can just get to a phone," I thought to myself. "I know they live somewhere in Vienna."

I collected our utensils and picked my steps through the humanity and straw to the check-in desk, where there were both a telephone and a telephone book. I was very nervous as I dialed the number and listened for the first ring.

"*Ja, bitte*," answered a young male voice, which I thought I recognized.

"Lixel, is that you? This is Frau Gegner, your foster mother from Cservenka." I heard a yell and the telephone drop. Then, after a few seconds, another voice came over the line.

"*Frau Gegner? Um Gottes Willen* (for goodness sakes), *nicht Sie, Frau Gegner, nein, nicht Sie* (not you! it can't be!)," said Mrs. Czeipeck over and over.

Between her outbursts, I told her that we had run from the Russian troops and had arrived only last night in Vienna. Upon hearing this, she repeated her moans: "No, not you, Mrs. Gegner; for goodness sakes, no, not you. You couldn't have lost everything." Her sympathetic outcry caused me to lose control, too.

"We'll be right over," she said. "We are within walking distance of the Opera House. We'll be right there. You are coming home with us. We'll be right there."

Blinking back tears, I hurried to give the good news to the children, who were waiting more or less patiently on the straw. Seeing how tightly Ibi was clasping Norbert, I felt a pang of compassion for her. Poor child; only ten years old and now deserted by her own parents. She had heard them say they would be back for her. "Back from where?" I murmured under my breath. If only women and children were in this location, they must be separating the sexes, I reasoned. It did not seem logical to me that they would find a refugee camp for married couples. But maybe they had no intention of staying in a refugee camp. Possibly, like me, they had friends in Vienna that they would try to contact. Maybe, too, Josef had made some kind of arrangement with the German officers who took the horses. They had talked intently for several minutes and from my knowledge of Josef, he persistently maneuvered to his advantage. "Who knows?" I said to myself, "he's probably already regained his horses and wagon for the trip home he is so positive about." In the meantime, though, *we* were going to a home.

"Guess what?" I said, making a place for myself on the straw. "We're going to Lixel's house." Lixel had been a big brother to Kurt and Gunther, and in spite of our situation, I had to laugh at the "whoopee" that came from the boys.

We got together all our earthly possessions, already less than we came with, and once more pushed our way to the front desk, where I received permission to leave for the day. Actually, no one cared if we left, but I was cautioned not to lose our identification cards or we would not be allowed to re-enter the building, and we would not get any food.

Outside on the sidewalk, we peered expectantly first up, then down the street, trying to pick out from the crowd people who obviously were not refugees, for refugees were still pouring into the city. Suddenly Gunther exclaimed, "Look! I think I see Lixel. Yes, yes, that *is* Lixel!" and he took off toward him.

What should have been a time of happy rejoicing lapsed quickly into tears. Lixel had laughed when he first caught sight of Gunther, but when he and his mother reached me, with only one look they began to cry—both of them.

"No, no, no, I can't believe it. This can't be happening, not to you!" Mrs. Czeipeck wailed as she embraced me. "What can I do for you? Only tell me, what can I do for you?"

Her genuine outpourings broke through what little control I held and we fell on each other for a time, oblivious of the curious stares of passersby. After some moments, my self-pity was brought up short: this lady was clean and sweet-smelling. I felt ashamed at having to meet her for the first time when I and the children were so dirty. And so my pride rescued the pathetic scene and we started our walk to their home: a condominium about three blocks away.

Upon entering the building, I felt even more out of place. Plush carpets and heavy velvet drapes, all in red, and the tastefully displayed paintings and sculpture recalled the luxury of a Vienna of another era. My agony grew even more acute when we stepped out of the elevator and into their penthouse, expensively decorated with pale green lace curtains, damask draperies, rich carpets and fine hardwood furniture covered with needlepoint.

Although it seemed ages ago, it was not too many days since I had lived in a similar setting; yet last night I had slept on the floor on straw, and all that I owned I now carried with me. Not only that, but Germans usually pride themselves on cleanliness—that certainly had been my upbringing—and here I stood, absolutely filthy, too dirty for these surroundings. None of us would dare sit even on the floor in her home, so when she asked once more what she could do for me, I did not hesitate.

"Please, only a bath. We haven't had a bath or changed our clothes since we left Cservenka." So, one after the other, I scrubbed the children and myself, and we dressed in the clean clothes which she gave us. I then gave her a ham shank, the last piece of meat we had, and together we cooked a good soup. But the soup was only the first course.

The dear woman was so grateful for the way we had provided free room and board for her son for six months and for all the food we had sent back with Lixel, that she wanted to repay us. I am certain that she spent all her month's ration stamps for us on that one day. We had special kinds of German buns and desserts, plus butter, eggs, coffee, all of which had long been rationed in Vienna. In fact, food was getting more and more scarce as the Allies' noose tightened on Hitler's Reich. Now it was my turn to be grateful, and I was: my morale had gotten a great boost and I was thankful and relieved that my children were eating some good, nourishing food.

Her husband, a high-ranking military officer, was away. She did not say much about the war—people in occupied countries like Austria were often afraid to speak their minds—but from her tone, I knew she was bitterly anti-Hitler. She could not understand why I felt I would be welcome or safe inside Germany, or why I would want to go there. She urged us to live with them, either in their Vienna apartment or in a summer home they owned nearby, until the end, which she was certain was near. When I told her Karl was with the

Yugoslavian *Volkssturm*, she groaned.

"We don't get much news because everything gets censored and radios are forbidden," she explained. "But we keep a short-wave radio hidden away and heard that all *Volkssturm* from sixteen to sixty years of age are ordered to report immediately for military duty. Hitler must be getting desperate."

"But what about the new weapon we keep hearing about?" I reminded her. She shrugged. "I know it looks like a lost cause—I kept telling Karl the same thing and I didn't want him to leave. I begged him to stay with our wagon train."

"It probably wouldn't matter now if he had stayed. This order is 'report or else.'" My mind jumped quickly to Josef and his friend from the Banat. "You *must* stay with us," she pressed again.

I should have been overjoyed with the offer, but a strange feeling came over me. I could not explain why, but I was convinced that I should return to the camp. Somehow this was not the place for me to stop. Maybe it was the knowledge that we would have to live on their rations. We, being refugees, would not be issued ration stamps along with the citizens of Vienna, and I could not in good conscience allow her to share her quota with five extra people. At the camp, we did have our food allotment, such as it was. And so, to her amazement, I declined the invitation. The children, too, while having such a good time with Lixel and his younger sister, had listened to our conversation, and the three oldest showed both surprise and disappointment at having to go back to the crowded camp to sleep on straw in a room covered with wall-to-wall people and where their pillow was stolen. Nevertheless, that is what we did, though not empty-handed. Mrs. Czeipeck washed our dirty clothes and also gave us some of theirs, plus some food, which I hoped I could hold on to until morning. They were beautiful people and gratefully generous, yet, illogical as it all seemed at the time, I could not stay there.

We spent our second night on the straw and in the morning got the news that we were being moved to Czechoslovakia. A massive bomb raid—the biggest yet—was expected in Vienna, and all refugees who chose to stay would be completely on their own with no ration cards and no food. I tried to call Mrs. Czeipeck to say goodbye, but I was not permitted to use the telephone because those at the desk were on alert.

As soon as we had finished eating our oatmeal and black bread, we were herded into a waiting train to begin our journey. I should have seriously questioned if I were doing the right thing, but I did not. Baffling as it was, I knew it was better to be jammed into the boxcar than to try to rejoin the family who had offered to take us in.

Thou has taken account of my wanderings;
Put my tears in Thy bottle . . . . (Psalm 56:8)

Chapter Seven

"Keep Going ! . . . Don't Stop!"

Our destination was Pilzen, Czechoslovakia, another step on my way—to where, I did not know. Geographically, Pilzen lies about two hundred miles northwest of Vienna in Sudetenland, which Hitler had annexed to Germany in 1938. Like Yugoslavia, Czechoslovakia had been an independent nation only since 1918, when the people declared themselves a republic following World War I. Prior to that, they had been part of Austria-Hungary. Many German-speaking people lived in the western part of the country, and as early as 1933 Nazi Germany began stirring up these Germans to demand independence from the rest of the nation. Then in 1938 at Munich, France and Great Britain agreed to Hitler's demands for parts of Czechoslovakia, an appeasement Hitler soon violated: in March 1938 he stormed into Prague, occupied the entire western half of Czechoslovakia, and set up a protectorate in the eastern half.

As we would learn, these Czechs, like the Russians, had one longing: the day they could get even with Hitler.

* * * * *

For three or four days, we rode in crowded boxcars like so much freight. Most of the children were noisy and fretful; the women, even when tending to their children, seemed preoccupied and depressed. A bench along three sides of the car gave sitting places for some; the rest sat on the floor. There was no room for moving about once the car was loaded. There were no windows, so we could not amuse ourselves with the passing scenery. Except for the crack around the door, there was no light in the car. As the air inside became increasingly stuffy, even breathing grew difficult.

Whenever bombs exploded nearby and the earth shook, the train stopped, often for hours at a time, until the engineer either got word or guessed that it was safe to proceed. It was especially dangerous near industrial sites, which were bombed day and night by the Allies, yet we could not always stay in the open countryside where we seemed to be safe. A couple times each day, the cars were opened so we could use the fields to relieve ourselves and get our ration of water and hunks of black bread smeared with white margarine.

In the dark confines of the boxcar, I could do little else than mentally review the hours since my separation from Sophia and Josef.

"Where did they go?" I asked myself repeatedly. "What will they do if they return to the campsite in Vienna and find Ibi gone? They really had no business leaving her with me in the first place. Anyway, I was told we would not be given food if I had elected to stay when a big raid was expected. . . . Then you should have gone back to the Czeipeck home. . . . No, somehow I know I should not have done that. 'Keep going! Don't stop!' That's what I keep hearing. Intuition? I don't know."

A young woman near me moaned softly, trying to soothe her whimpering baby. She was all alone, except for the infant. For a few moments, I studied her face. The atmosphere, murky as it was, could not mute the desolation I saw there, but as there was little I could do for her, I returned to my inner world.

"Karl . . . where are you, Karl? . . . Are you riding in a troop train someplace? . . . Where? . . . The Western Front? . . . The *Volkssturm* had to report for duty. Why? . . . Is Hitler so low on troops that he has to use boys and old men? Is Mrs. Czeipeck right? Is it really all over for Germany? She's convinced that it is. . . . She thought I was crazy to want to get into Germany where our ancestors came from. . . . Oh, I don't know what to think or what to hope . . . ." The earth trembled again, this time violently. "What if a bomb hits the train? Maybe that would be better after all—to be killed right now and be done with everything. . . . NO!" The word escaped aloud.

"Mamma? What's the matter, Mamma? Are you all right?" Gunther's soft-spoken concern magnified the horror of my last thought. As I instinctively reached for him, I reminded myself, "I must keep going . . . just keep going. O God, please . . . help me."

"Yes, Gunther," I replied, after a few seconds of patting his arm. "I'm all right. Nothing is the matter. I guess I was dreaming."

At Budweiss, a community south of Pilzen, some refugees were taken from the train. After the rest of us arrived at the Pilzen station, we were put on buses for a ride of several miles to what looked like a cheaply-constructed military camp of about twenty-five, one-story, wooden barracks. It was late afternoon, and those of us who already were processed were ordered to get in line right away for dinner. Those without refugee identification joined other lines to get registered before they were allowed to eat.

Each outdoor "buffet," a large table covered with make-shift canopy and with a huge pot at each end, served about three barracks. As we filed by on both sides, Czech stewards contemptuously ladled steaming potato soup into our extended metal cups. They did not seem to care if the soup hit the cup or not, and several of the women cried out as the scalding liquid spilled over their bare hands. Whenever this happened, the stewards muttered something. I did not understand their language, but I did not need to. Their eyes said it all: hate. I got an extra cup for Norbert and herded the children away from the table as quickly as possible. To keep our mouths from being burned, we sipped the watery soup slowly, all the while passing the hot metal cup from one hand to the other. Fluids cooled fast in the chill of October's end, so by the time I had finished drinking mine, Norbert's was ready, and he gulped the runny soup as if he had not eaten for days.

Dinner over, we were randomly assigned to quarters—about fifty to each cold, flimsy barracks. Here, however, unlike in Vienna, we would have a choice of where to sleep: a mound of hay on the floor or a bunk (a few of which lined one wall).

"Mamma, what's that?" Kurt said, pointing to something in the middle of the room. The boys had never seen a potbelly stove and it fascinated them. Another plus: heat. Although we were disappointed to learn that toilets and washbasins were in a separate building, after four days in a crowded, dark boxcar, this place seemed almost luxurious, and we could now walk around without stepping on someone. Others must have felt the same way.

"You know, this really has possibilities," one of the women volunteered cheerfully, twirling around and gesturing with her arms. "Tomorrow we can get a fire going and fill up some of the drafty places with straw. Does anyone have any suggestions for curtains?"

It was amazing what a little hot soup could do, and she got

several lighthearted replies before we turned our attention to who should get the bunks. A few older women were willing to crowd two to a bunk, and we unselfishly deferred to each other for the rest of them. Gunther and little Norbert shared one while Ibi, Kurt, and I made hay mattresses on the floor. I was so tired that even the hay felt good, and I sank into a dreamless sleep.

Everyone must have been exhausted that night, for no one awoke until the bell rang, which, as we discovered, was used to announce meals. But there were urgent matters to take care of before we ate, so hundreds of us scurried to the one building with the plumbing. The long wait was anxious, and several wandered to the back of the building. But they did not lose much privacy after all, because inside we were also in the open: no doors anywhere. Cold water came from the faucets but there was no soap, so the best we could do was rinse our hands and faces. We would not be able to bathe or wash clothes.

While waiting in line, I met women from Rumania and parts of Yugoslavia, all *Volksdeutsche*. In the huge group I also noticed several old men, a few of them talking with old women, apparently their wives. "You're lucky," I thought to myself. They would not be housed together, but they could see each other most of the time.

As we hurried back to our serving table, I heard a coarse "You get in line when the bell rings or go without food! We're not standing out here to wait hand and foot on everybody." We got more of the same language, mixed with curses, at our own station plus a repeat of contemptuous service. I grew uneasy. To have hate directed at me was a new experience, and I voiced my misgivings as we moved inside to finish our eating.

"Oh, it makes them feel superior to bully a few Germans. But don't worry; they wouldn't dare do anything to us. Hitler has control of Czechoslovakia and he won't let anything happen to Germans," said one from my country.

"That's right," agreed another. "Remember what they told us— that we'd be away from our homes only a short time. Germany will win this war." A few others chimed the same note, but I noticed the one from Rumania said nothing.

"We'll be safe here, so let's make the best of it," said the cheerful one of the night before. "Start plugging up some of the cracks around the windows and help me get a fire going in this stove."

"Surprise!" piped up another. "I've got a small, portable hot plate that I've managed to hang on to, and here's an electric outlet. If it works, we can heat water and maybe even find something to put in it . . . tea, coffee, cocoa!"

An appropriate cheer erupted, completing the theatrics. A spirit of gaiety filled the room, and Kurt, Gunther, and Ibi joined the crew filling cracks while I, still apprehensive, tried to enlist Norbert in some make-believe of building a house out of straw.

The activity made the time pass quickly and the bell rang once again, summoning us to the same hate-filled table. The meal consisted of very watery potato soup, hard, black break (old but nourishing), chicory, and milk for the very young children. Curious about our surroundings and wondering if others from Cservenka were in the camp, after eating I set out with the children to do some exploring. Others apparently had the same idea, and it was encouraging to hear a shout every once in a while as people recognized each other—either personally or by responding to names of towns as they were called out. I latched on to a few from Cservenka, and although I had not been acquainted with them previously, they all knew the Gegner name. Before long, we were exchanging stories of our escapes and news about the war.

"So Gegner Karl is with the *Volkssturm*," said one elderly man. "He's probably going to the Western Front. I heard some rumors that Hitler is planning a big show of strength out there. I'm seventy, so I didn't have to report."

I met another piece of news: Belgrade had been taken on October 20 by the combined forces of the Red Army and Tito's Partisans. Convinced that the fighting had stopped in Yugoslavia, many said they were considering returning to their homes right away.

"Do you really believe the Russians will welcome you if you return?" I asked, surprised at myself for speaking up.

"Sure, why not?" replied the seventy-year-old man. "We haven't done anything to the Russians. Russians might take it out on Hitler's Germans, but not on us."

"But haven't you noticed how the Czech guards look at us? They hate us. And they know we don't come from Germany," I retorted. "I think the safest place for us is in Germany."

"Inside Germany? No, as soon as the fighting is over in the Batschka and the Banat, it will be safe for us to go home. And it probably won't matter too much for us which way the war goes either. If Germany wins, well, we're Germans. If not, since both Tito and the king are against Germany, no one should bother us. We're citizens of Yugoslavia."

"I agree," added a woman of about forty. "And these Czechs don't actually hate us. They're just upset at having to take care of so many refugees."

"You've maybe heard the rumor that the Czecks will kill every last German they can get their hands on just as soon as Germany loses?" guessed the old man, correctly. "In every crowd you always find a crackpot who wants to intimidate people. It's nonsense anyway. Civilized people don't butcher innocent refugees."

I had already seen what some "civilized" people could do. Yet these seemed confident of their safety and I know they thought I was being very silly with my talk of trying to get into Germany. They all planned to stay where they were and leave for home as soon as they could. I, on the other hand, began to take my first steps toward Germany.

The next day I approached the guard to ask for a pass. They were easy to get, and sightseeing was the usual reason given for leaving camp. For many, however, the real reason for getting off the compound was to engage in the activities of the black market, and I am quite sure the guards knew it. As in Vienna, the problem was not in leaving the camp but in getting back in, and all identification tags were carefully checked. Without them, we lost our place to sleep and our food.

Pass in hand, I took the children to the barracks where smoke was belching from the potbelly stove, told them to wait inside until I returned, and set out for the Headquarters Building a short distance from the compound.

"Why?" barked the officer at the desk. "Why do you want to go to Germany?"

Why? I did not answer right away because I did not really know why myself.

"Do you have relatives there who will take care of you?" he wanted to know.

"No."

"Then you better stay here. All you can expect is another refugee camp," he replied bruskly, "and it might be worse in Germany than it is here."

"I don't care. I must get into Germany."

"I'll have to think about it." With this, he turned aside.

My disappointment must have shown, because as I entered the barracks, several of the women took one look at me and said, one after the other: "No luck? Well, what did you expect? You don't really think they will let you go, do you? Anyway, why risk more danger when we are safe right here? The war will soon be over and we can go back home." Common sense saw the logic of their arguments, but something inside me was saying, "Don't listen to them. Don't stop here. Keep going."

As soon as breakfast was over the next day, I stood again at the desk at Headquarters. There was a different face this time. "I'd like papers to enter Germany–for my children and me," I explained. Again came the question Why? And again, because I was reluctant to say "Well, you see, officer, there's a voice inside me that keeps telling me to keep going, and now it tells me to try to get into Germany," I only repeated my same request: "Please, I'd like papers to enter Germany–for my children and me." He shrugged his shoulders.

"You'll have to buy train tickets. Do you have money?"

"I have Yugoslavian currency."

"That's no good here and I don't know if we can exchange it. I'll check on it." And he turned his attention to someone else.

With that bit of encouragement, I repeated the routine the next morning, only to be met by the first face. "You again? You still want to go to Germany? Germany gets bombed every day. You are safer here."

When I told him I had money for my fare and that another man was checking to see if I could exchange the currency, he dismissed me with "I don't know anything about that." So the runaround at Headquarters followed by jibes from those at the barracks continued. But the cycle was interrupted by the appearance of Sophia and Josef.

They burst into the barracks that afternoon, very angry. "My child!" Sophia yelled at me as she grabbed Ibi. "What do you think you are doing with my child? We've looked all over for you. I told you to wait for us in Vienna, but when we got there, you were gone."

Stunned by her outburst, I told of the expected bomb raid and that we had all been ordered to leave and that we would get no food if we stayed.

"Well, the camp had not been bombed when we were there," she said, but in a slightly softer tone. "We're heading for home now. We've heard that it's safe. You and the boys come with us."

"What?" It was my turn to exclaim. "I don't believe it's safe. There must be Russians and Partisans everywhere. The Germans have lost in Belgrade. How does that make it safe for returning *Volksdeutsche*? No, it's not safe there. I'm going to Germany." Josef and Sophia, hearing these assessments of the war from the lips of one who had always been protected and non-political, stared at me with their mouths open. Even I was amazed at my own voice.

"Kristina! have you lost your mind? You can't go into Germany all by yourself!" It was Josef's turn to explode. "A woman alone with three young boys and without even townspeople to watch out for each other! You'll be asking for far more trouble than you can handle. And what would Karl say? Think about him for a minute. No, you come with us. We've been told it's safe enough to start back."

They then explained that they had gone to Silesia where they met several *Volksdeutsche* from Yugoslavia. They had agreed to travel home together by commercial train. Josef and Sophia had gotten separated from the group when they went back to Vienna, but they had plans to make connections again. Refugee camps were filling up rapidly, they reported, and those in charge did not object if people left, thus giving them fewer mouths to feed.

"I'm going to Germany," I insisted. "I can't give you a good reason. I only know I must. I'll be welcome among real Germans. I'm of their stock. I knew the day I left Cservenka that my home there was gone forever. I'm glad you got here in time to get Ibi, though. I'd rather not be responsible for her."

"Pappa," interrupted Ibi. "We had a chance to live with some rich people in Vienna, but Aunty Kristina made us go back to the camp."

My sister and her husband stared at me again. "Come on," said Josef. "There will be a train here in a few hours and I want to make certain everything is in order." And so we parted. They thought I was a crazy fool. I thought they were gullible to be taken in by propaganda.

I was sorry to separate with strained feelings between us, but the next day I was back at Headquarters, where I met another face but the same routine. Discouraged yet undaunted I kept returning, day after day for about ten days. Finally, I grew exasperated. I took my money, approached the desk, and demanded an exchange of my currency into German marks and train tickets to Germany.

Startled by my brash manner, the man whose face I had seen before took a couple steps backward while his eyes reviewed me thoughtfully. I lived an eternity in that one minute. At last he lowered his gaze and said, wearily, "All right, lady, you can go to Germany. To Forchheim, Germany."

There was a refugee camp there.

ONCE A REFUGEE

Whom have I in heaven but Thee?
And besides Thee, I desire nothing on earth.
My flesh and my heart may fail;
But God is the strength of my heart and
my portion forever. (Psalm 73:25-26)

Chapter Eight

Unwanted: Refugees

Running at top speed back to the barracks, I bounded into the room just in time for morning "coffee," which was brewing in the tin cans we had managed to round up. The used chicory grounds salvaged from previous meals did not have much flavor, but the hot fluid was safe to drink, and the ritual furnished a link with the orderly lives we had all left behind.

"I can go! I can leave for Germany tomorrow!" I shouted, slamming the door behind me. "See, here are my papers!" The women stood by, astonished, while three boys, huddled together near the stove to keep warm, jumped up to hug me.

"Mamma, will Daddy be waiting in Germany for us?" Kurt and Gunther never let up with questions about their father and I was often at a loss about how to encourage their childlike hope without setting them up for possible disappointment. I said that I was not sure where their father was but that he probably got the mail we sent regularly and knew where we were. Karl had given me his military number, so I did have an address for him.

"As soon as we send him our address in Germany, we should start to get mail," I assured them both. "We probably haven't gotten his answers to our letters because we have been moving around so much." My explanation seemed to satisfy them. Little did they guess how much I needed to believe my own words.

My victory with the authorities caused a few of the women to wonder if they should try a similar tactic; however, they soon squelched the idea in favor of common sense. Winter was soon upon them. Here in Pilzen, they had not been bombed, they had adequate food to keep alive, they had a roof over their heads, and they were free to move about outside. Such conditions made survival likely. Unless ordered to move, they would mark time in Czechoslovakia until the war ended. I, on the other hand, was eager to be on my way. So, to help the day move faster, I wrote a letter to Mrs. Czeipeck, bringing her up to date and urging her to write to us in Forchheim. I also wrote again to Karl and posted both letters as we left the camp the next afternoon.

It did not take long to pack. Except for the clothes on our backs, all we had to carry was one small satchel and a blanket each for Gunther and Kurt plus my big, leather purse, which contained my jewelry and money. I had asked for, and received, a few extra hunks of bread at the noon meal, because without ration cards I would not be able to buy food no matter how much money I had. I could get food only at refugee camps.

Although the sky was heavily overcast and drizzling, a couple of the women with their children accompanied us for the walk out to the highway which ran a few blocks from the compound and saw us off on the bus with wishes of good luck. The train would not be leaving until evening, but I wanted to get to the station in plenty of time to buy our tickets and while the November daylight was still with us. Knowing I would not be given a fair rate for my money, I had exchanged only what I needed for our passage. I was holding on to the rest of my Yugoslavian and Hungarian currency which, as it turned out, would serve me well later.

The train was crowded. Not only were languages being spoken which I could understand, but there were others which I could not recognize at all. Yet even in this international mix of travelers who could still pay their own ways, the same vacant look of despair and hopelessness prevailed. Fortunately, the children and I got one seat, which had to do for the four of us. I held Norbert on my lap and Gunther and Kurt squeezed together next to me.

* * * * *

Total darkness had settled as the train slowly made its way up into the hilly terrain of the Bohemian Forest, and I thought, "I've been here before . . . but it wasn't on a train. . . . It was a sleigh . . . on my hill near Cservenka . . . beauty . . . and danger . . . ." The only light came from flashlights beamed occasionally at the track by the engineers. Because no light was permitted inside the train, the landscape was clearly visible through the window, which I slid open just a little and, pressing my nose into the crack, I breathed deeply of the clear, pure air. It already had the smell of snow. Whenever the moon peeked through a hole in the clouds, its rays revealed snow-covered mountain tops in the distance. To match the quiet of the outdoors, human voices also hushed. Between these two stillnesses intruded the noise of the train, the reminder in our plight that there was no peace. The entire world was at war, a war which my sympathetic response to a sleeping nature could not still. My thoughts flashed back again, this time to the Armenian village, and I yearned for the sweet perfume of the peace I had breathed there . . . a soul peace that allowed no intrusion.

* * * * *

Germany still guarded its 1937 border with Czechoslovakia even though the line had been extended to include the Sudetenland. Immediately, as the train came to a stop here, it was boarded by several Nazi officers with the command, "Papers!" In a few cases, where apparently not everything was *in Ordnung*, the passengers were promptly put under arrest and forcibly removed from the train. I was shaking badly when my turn came to hand the officer my papers. What if what I had been issued was not "in order?" Besides the registration number I had been assigned in Vienna which designated me as a refugee, I had only a paper which released me from the camp at Pilzen and bore the stamp "Forchheim." He looked at the paper, then at me, then at the paper again, and sneered, "Refugees! Yugoslavian refugees! What's the matter with them in Pilzen? Now they're sending riffraff into Germany." When he said "riffraff," he turned to face me squarely. The instant his steel eyes met mine, I felt my momentary flush of anger turn chalk white. With a haughty laugh, he moved to the next seat.

Completely unnerved, I stared out the window, trying to regain my composure. I was thankful the boys were too sleepy to have caught the significance of the officer's language. I kept telling myself over and over again that no real German would treat me this way. The Nazi officer represents only an insensitive military and not the common German, I tried to convince myself. After about an hour of watching mountain forest pass before my eyes and being rocked by the train's motion, I began to relax. Yet I barely dared to reflect on what could have been my fate.

So determined had I been to get out of Czechoslovakia that I had toyed with the idea of taking off on my own, without trying to get papers. No one checked who left the camp at Pilzen. There, the only concern was who entered the grounds. So I could have wandered off and made it as far as the border. However, as I had seen, without authorization to travel in a strange country, which Germany was to me, I would not have gotten by the border check point—not even with a wagon load of Nazi uniforms. And, I shuddered to think of it, I would have faced arrest.

About midnight we rolled into the Nuremberg station, completing the first leg of the trip to Forchheim. Here we would lay over until morning when we would finish the last thirty miles or so. We joined the crowds inside and found a place on a bench where we ate our bread, after which the boys went back to sleep. Trains continued to enter the station. As the benches filled up, people began to sit on the floor near the walls to try to get some sleep. Blackouts continued; the room was dark.

Around two o'clock the sirens began. Then, over the loudspeaker:

"*Achtung! Achtung!* Everyone! Proceed immediately to the lower floor of the station. Move quickly. Do not panic!"

Already we could hear and feel the bombs thunder around us. As the lightning from each explosion illumined the room, I could see panic on faces. People jumped up, pushed and shoved their way to the side staircase leading to tracks below. Their screams heightened the hysteria but failed to drown out the siren's constant wailing and the loudspeaker's barked commands. Gunther and Norbert awoke with the siren, and I quickly put Karl's leather jacket on Gunther. Kurt stayed asleep. When he slept, he slept. I was trying to carry him and Norbert too, all the while being herded along in the frantic mob. What a sight we must have made. Karl's jacket, so long it dragged on the floor, almost smothered Gunther. He looked like a bear carrying a satchel and two blankets. I was not able to hold on to both boys for more than a few steps.

"Kurt! Wake up!" I yelled, letting him slide from my arms. He was able to stand on his feet and while he rubbed his eyes and looked around totally confused, I said again, "Kurt! Stay awake and grab hold of my skirt and don't let go. Come on now, you stay on one side of Mamma. Gunther, you stay on the other. Don't let go! Hang on with all your might!" We did not have to decide our direction; that was determined by the crowd.

Suddenly hundreds of us were moving down the stairs, where we met with near disaster. As some legs could navigate better than others, the flow of the crowd grew uneven. Some people lagged behind; others almost jumped over those in front of them. Kurt, asleep again even though on his feet, had relaxed his grip on my skirt and, before I realized what had happened, was swept aside. Choked with fear and trying desperately to turn around and force my way against the oncoming mass, I screamed, "He'll be trampled to death! Please . . . don't trample my child!" As if miraculously, the people parted and there at the end of the corridor, stood Kurt, now fully awake and reaching toward me.

We came to a huge bunker under the railway station and took our places—some on benches, most on the bare floor. For nearly two hours we huddled together in stony silence as the bombs screamed through the air and exploded on industrial sites which surrounded the station. Although I had panicked for those few minutes on the stairs, here in the bunker, even as I watched the huge supporting pillars wave back and forth as the bombs pummeled the area, I was no longer afraid. An inner calm I could not then explain was beginning to take hold of me, and I was confident we would be safe.

With the "all clear" signal, we made our way in orderly fashion to the main floor in ample time for the train. At Forchheim, those of us assigned to the refugee camp were met by a big nurse, a member of a disaster relief crew, who escorted us to a receiving station. Here, we were given breakfast of soup and bread, and Gunther and Kurt watched as Norbert drank his milk. The mat of welcome encouraged me. Shortly we were placed on buses for the trip to the camp. The large, five-story building looked nice from the outside, but as we entered what was formerly a school, a familiar scene lay before us.

The few hundred people sitting on the floor on straw had lost everything, just as we had. Scattered here and there were a few suitcases, some dirty blankets, and some outer garments. We got our little space on the floor, maybe five by six feet, and started all over again. We got in line for our food, a steady diet of beet soup with oatmeal. The oatmeal was old, and fat, white worms floated on top of the gruel. As days passed and our hunger increased, we gulped them down almost greedily. In Germany, food was more scarce than it had been in either Austria or Czechoslovakia.

The schoolhouse had some sinks for washing, and people had strung a line from one end of the room to the other on which wash of all kinds was hanging. So the cold room was also damp. In addition, children were usually screaming and there was absolutely no privacy. My boys saw things they never should have seen. Moreover, the straw had been used by others—from the looks of it, by many others. It was filthy, and with the filth came lice.

It was hardest for the children, and their cries of "Mamma, I'm hungry" broke my heart. So I left the boys alone in the camp and went begging, not in the town but in the rural places surrounding Forchheim, for I had always known farmers to be generous. I saw how poor the German people were because of the war, but they had more than I had. Yet one after the other they hurled verbal abuse at me and slammed the door in my face.

"We don't have anything to give you. If you had had something, you never would have left your homeland. Why did you come to our poor Germany? We don't want you!" They even called me a gypsy. A gypsy! I had been one of the wealthiest women in Cservenka. Being called a derogatory name was a bigger blow to my pride than begging was. I was begging, after all, for the sake of my children. I felt sorry for myself and cried all the way back to the camp. When I saw the children running to greet me as I entered the big room, I quickly dried by face.

"Mamma, did you bring anything?" they all asked. In my apron I had a few pieces of hard bread which someone had thrown away. We went together to the bellystove to warm the bits so they would not be so tough to eat. My routine of begging went on for weeks.

Although it was well into December, and although I had written to Karl and others, we received no mail. In the meantime, the boys, especially Norbert, got lice. He had the least hair, but had the most lice. Great big ones crawled all over him. The little washing we were allowed to do was of little benefit when we had to return to the same infested straw. The children grew more pale by the day and were showing physical signs of malnutrition. Even more ominous was

Gunther's cough.

* * * * *

In view of what was happening, I should certainly have
questioned my decision to leave both Mrs. Czeipeck and the camp in
Czechoslovakia. But I did not. Of course I was concerned, at times
apprehensive, about the health of the boys. Yet I was given strength
to face each new day and I held to the assurance that I had done the
right thing and that times would get better. In terms of material
wealth, I had lost more than many people accumulate in a lifetime. It
has been said before, and many can testify from personal experience,
that it often takes a loss to force people to make thoughtful inventory
of their lives. I was on the threshold of doing so with mine.

* * * * *

Gunther had tuberculosis. His exposure to Georg during the first
days of our escape plus his getting overtired and his lack of
nourishing food had their predictable result. I finally had to put him
in a sanatorium. We could all visit him occasionally because we were
given a pass to ride the bus. Then Norbert got space in the hospital
for his condition with lice. I was thankful that for the time being they
would get good food. In fact, Gunther's appearance improved rapidly
and he was soon sent back to the camp. Also, Norbert's lice were
checked. Through it all, Kurt alone stayed healthy-looking. Always
happy, jolly, and independent, he never complained.

We were all together again in the schoolhouse, filthy straw and
all, when we had an unusually big air raid. On a Saturday evening
while I was bathing the boys in an old-fashioned tub, the sirens
wailed.

"Down! Down! Everyone get down in the shelter!" yelled the
guard as he entered the washroom filled with scrubbed, wet, young
bodies. "There's no time to dress. Move . . . NOW!"

I did not want my boys to run naked in the cold, particularly
Gunther with his tuberculosis, so I grabbed what was at hand—a big
blanket. I quickly spread it out and ordered the boys to sit in the
middle. Then I pulled the four corners up over my shoulders and
dragged the huge knapsack across the floor and down what seemed
like endless flights of stairs. The boys screamed as their bottoms

bounced from step to step. But their cries were mixed with giggles. Whenever I passed a window I could see the phosphorus coming from the planes and bursting into flame before it hit the ground. All kinds of fire coming down from the sky brought on another wave of panic among the refugees. Industries around us were the targets and even though no bombs hit the schoolhouse, we learned that people caught outside actually became human torches. Following the raid, there were numerous fires on the outskirts of the town. The next day, as the boys and I watched the smoke still rising from the burning rubble, I wondered what happened to the marvelous weapon that was supposed to end the war quickly.

Soon it would be Christmas, that joyful time of family togetherness, but I had nothing to be joyful about. Karl and I were separated and I did not know if he was even alive. I had only myself and the boys . . . and the lice and bedbugs. We were full of bites which bled from the constant itching and scratching. Christmas . . . a time for giving and receiving presents. Gradually an idea took shape in my mind.

When the time of day came for my trek to beg or scrounge around for extra food for the boys, I started off as usual, but this time I gathered up my courage and went into Forchheim and approached the *Bürgermeister*. He patiently listened while I described conditions inside the schoolhouse–the filth, wormy food, lack of washing facilities, and so forth–and Gunther's illness, which was aggravated by the cold dampness.

"Couldn't you give us one little room so I can have privacy with my children and keep them clean?" I pleaded. "I don't care how small it is." I knew it required the permission of the mayor to live in the community outside the refugee camp and also that only he could grant ration cards so I could get food and cook our meals. He viewed me for a moment or two, then spoke kindly.

"There is a man and his wife whose only son is in the service," he said. "His room is vacant. You can have that. The house is in Wiesenthau right outside of Forchheim. I'll notify the people and have papers made up for you."

I could hardly keep from crying. His door was not slammed in my face. He then said to come back the next day with our things and he would point out the way. It would be a long walk, he added, but if we started out right after the morning meal he thought we would have enough energy to make it.

Arriving in the small village of about fifty homes, the boys and I eagerly looked for the right house, which we soon found. Our reception, however, was far from cordial. In fact, she absolutely refused to let us in. Another door slammed!

Not knowing what to do, I inquired of the nearest neighbor. She was sympathetic and told me to go to the village Justice of the Peace. From him we received a police escort, who forced the door open to us.

"We all have to share our homes and whatever we have with the refugees," insisted the officer.

"Well, I want no part of it," she retorted. "I don't care about refugees. The whole bunch of you should have stayed in your own country." No matter how nice I tried to be to her, she continued to be very mean. I know she was worried about her son, and I could understand that. But it was not our fault that we had to leave everything. I wanted peace, and I wanted to be a help to her, but she would not let me. "And don't you ever come into my bathroom or come close to us," she yelled, storming from the room.

The small room had a bellystove. The children slept together in the one bed; I slept on a cot. The outhouse was some distance away.

By this time everyone in the Catholic town was decorating for Christmas. Fortunately, the neighbor who had helped us the day we arrived took an interest in us and invited us to spend Christmas Eve with them. We made our way through the winter fairyland to their home and were welcomed into a warm room scented with candles, kerosene lamps, a wood-burning stove, and the newly-cut fir tree, brightly decorated. Because of the food scarcity, there were none of the traditional goodies, nor did we exchange any presents. But these people shared what they had, and, most important of all, they gave of themselves. Other people in the village were like the people we stayed with; they did not want to share. This Catholic family was different.

As we sang together the carols telling of God's gift of His only Son, the words spoke to me, and I thanked the Lord of Heaven for His mercy to me. I did have something to be joyful about. For the first time in years, I actually prayed. I don't remember all that I said, but I knew I had to get my life closer to God. I had been far away. "Trust Me, Kristina," He seemed to say. For me, the moment was sacred.

Christmas! The Prince of Peace was born in Bethlehem. There was no peace on earth, but there was peace in this home—Armenian village peace—and I did not want the evening to end.

* * * * *

1945 dawned with incendiary bombing in the distance continuing to light the night skies. No mail came for me, and our landlady's attitude got more and more nasty. She would not permit me to do anything, so totally did she despise me. The children, too, were getting on her nerves because, as their health improved, they did not like to be cooped up inside. But with all the snow and our lack of proper clothing, we could not spend much time outside. Especially difficult was our daily chore of gathering sticks for our bellystove. We were limited to the small pieces which had fallen from trees and were not allowed to cut firewood. Not that we could anyway, because the landlady refused me use of their ax. Each day, for as long as we could tolerate the cold, we carefully searched every inch of ground for twigs. All property was privately owned and people were understandably jealous about what belonged to them, so I took care to obey the rules. On one occasion, though, we were reported to the authorities for picking up twigs that were too big. I was humiliated. I was also discouraged at having my offers to help always spurned.

I went again, therefore, to the kind *Bürgermeister*, who well remembered the icy reception the boys and I had gotten. "She doesn't want us," I answered, when he asked if things were going smoothly. "Please, can you find us another place?"

"All right," he said. "You go to Willersdorf on the other side of Forchheim, on the west side. A couple there is willing to take someone in to help with the farming. Are you willing to work?" I was willing. Until the end of the war, that would be our home.

Meanwhile, unknown to me, the Battle of the Bulge had taken place in Belguim and Allied forces were pushing into western Germany: Hitler's use there of the *Volkssturm* had bought him only one month. And in the north, Russian troops had poured into Silesia from Poland and had overcome what was left of that German defense after Hitler had ordered the bulk of those forces into Hungary in his attempt to hold Budapest. Thus Silesia fell easily into Russian hands. We would later learn the cost of this Russian "liberation" to some members of our wagon train from Cservenka.

It was early February 1945. In three months, there would be a victory in Europe. It would not be Germany's.

And in the shadow of Thy wings I will take refuge,
Until destruction passes by. (Psalm 57:1b)

Chapter Nine

Countdown to Defeat

For our move to Willersdorf, the *Bürgermeister* enlisted a farmer to give us a ride in his cow wagon. Although I was reminded of the sad day we left Cservenka, I was grateful to be spared a very long walk through freezing snow. The boys, of course, thought the trip was great fun even though they wished old Bossy could gallop instead of amble along. We meandered through the rolling hills typical of Bavaria. On the other side of Forchheim, however, the scene changed dramatically. A thick forest bordered the west side of the town, opening into a valley and flat farmland which was the village of Willersdorf, one of several small villages surrounding Forchheim. We entered a neighborhood obviously poorer than that of Wiesenthau and approached the house which became our home: an unpainted wooden structure, two stories high, located on a corner. Across the dirt street was the Catholic church.

We stopped in front and three people came out of the house and moved shyly toward the cart with wishes of welcome. What a difference from our previous reception! I learned later that they had been very curious to see us, as word had spread even to them about our ill-treatment. We had gained some notoriety because we were the first refugees to be housed in a private home in the Forchheim area, and these folk led such isolated lives that to them it was as if we had come from another planet. They reminded me of the poor Serbian and Hungarian peasants I had seen. The man and wife, Herr and Frau Haan, were probably about fifty, and her spinster sister, *Tante* (Aunt) Rettle, was about ten years their senior. But they looked ninety, and it was apparent that they were not used to bathing regularly.

Entering the house, we were shown to our upstairs room, the best one in the poorly-kept house. However, I sensed their genuine welcome and concern for a stranger with three little boys, and for the first time since I had walked out of my own home, the dirt and lice did not seem to matter. In our room stood nothing but two beds, one big, one small. But we had a view over the entire village. I still had our two blankets, and, for additional covers, we were given a few pieces of what in Cservenka would have passed for rags.

The first few days were unpleasantly cold because we had no heat. I was, however, eligible for a stove through the International Refugee Organization. And such a stove it turned out to be! A brand new wood-burning range, with coal also provided. Now we would be warm and I could cook. We had our ration cards and could get some food at a small grocery store not far away. Although there was not enough food to satisfy hunger, we would not starve, and spring and the growing season were ahead.

At this time, my Hungarian money proved helpful. I paid the Haans handsomely every month. These people could not read or write, but their one son had some education, and, whenever he would visit, his parents would pass the money on to him. I think he was able to make profitable trades with it. In return, they were very good to me. Occasionally, in the evening, I would hear footsteps on the stairway followed by a soft knock on the door.

"Pst! Frau Gegner!" There would be *Tante* Rettle bringing me an egg or half a liter of milk or a small piece of ham.

Gradually I cleaned up our quarters. With my ration card I got washing powder and soap, and religiously, every Saturday, I scrubbed the floor in our room, the hallway, and the stairs, soon restoring rough, dirty planks to their original golden grain. As a child I had indeed learned to do it right! The Haans respected me for keeping up their house.

Gunther and Kurt were happy about our move because they were immediately placed in school where they kept busy during the day and met children their age. Also, for the first time in years, I started to attend church. At first, it was the Catholic church across the street, where the bells peeled every morning summoning the faithful to prayers. The Haans were pleased when I accepted their invitation to attend mass with them. In fact, the whole village warmed to us as they saw my willingness to become part of them. However, I was not comfortable with Catholic forms of worship, so when I learned of a Protestant church in the next village, we walked there, joining with the Catholics only when the weather was bad. The boys liked to go to church.

As for me, what I had felt on Christmas Eve was having a continuing effect. The thought haunted me: "Something is missing from your life, Kristina," and I knew it concerned my relationship to God. I had always believed God existed and that He had sent Jesus His Son to be the Savior. Did I need a Savior? I wondered. Had I not done quite well with my life, and without any help from God? Recent events making me a political refugee were not my fault. God would not hold me responsible for international war. I had no control or influence there. Yet somehow I knew that was not the issue. Slowly, ever so slowly, I was coming to realize that it had been my deliberate choice to be a refugee spiritually. Like the prodigal son, I was beginning to come to my senses.

I wished then that I had our Bible which had been stolen in Austria. The Haans did not have a Bible, but they loaned me a catechism. The doctrine was different from what I had studied for my confirmation, but I read it to the boys anyway. God was tugging and I was reaching out, but what He wanted from me I could not fully grasp.

* * * * *

The weather was getting noticeably warmer and one day Herr Haan began to plow his fields. I had been used to long days of hard work when I was a girl, but I had never helped with the plowing because my father had a tractor and plowed with modern machinery. These Bavarian farmers still used oxen and soon I was walking behind a yoke, guiding the heavy plow through the wet earth, with Norbert following after with his stick. He was copying Herr Haan, who walked in front leading the oxen. Frau Haan and *Tante* Rettle came behind with seed, which was put into the ground by hand— more backbreaking work. My father, even twenty years earlier, had used machines for planting. I was exhausted at the day's end, but it felt good to be doing something worthwhile and I looked forward to the fresh vegetables we would soon be eating. As neighbors saw me working in this manner in the fields, they greeted me with enthusiasm, and I knew they completely accepted me. These open doors in Willersdorf, however humble, were the sign to me that not all the world had gone bad.

My favored status as the lone refugee was soon to end as refugees began arriving from Silesia. These people, mostly Polish *Volksdeutsche*, had fled before the Russian Army crossed the Oder River. Before long, every family in the village was housing refugees. Some of them, having long-since thrown morals to the winds, quickly gained a very bad reputation, spoiling relationships with the villagers for all of us.

Despite the air of secrecy which hung over the area as these farmers were afraid to voice their suspicions about the war, this growing influx of refugees was itself grist for the rumor mill. Moreover, stories of all kinds began spreading as refugees whispered among themselves, usually when they met while getting food rations at the stores in Forchheim.

One day while I was there, a chill gripped my heart when I heard the word "Jews." I moved closer to the one speaking. "Have you heard that?" she was asking. "It can't be, but that's what we heard in Silesia . . . that they make lampshades out of Jewish skin!"

"What nonsense!" put in another. "That's just talk." We all nodded. It could not be true.

On another occasion, I overheard others talking very quietly about the fate of the super weapon that so many Germans were pinning their hopes on. The story was being circulated that the project was sabotaged by German military who were betraying their own government because they had concluded Hitler was a madman. Villagers also must have heard these stories, and although they did not talk of these things, their faces became sadder and more drawn as they must have guessed, along with us refugees, that the end was near.

We did not know it then, but the Americans were pushing down hard upon our area from the north in what was to be the final offensive of the war, and I did not know, of course, that riding among these very troops was a man who would be important to me many years in the future. Their main swath was cut southward and slightly east of us as they fought their way toward Austria, but we could hear shooting whenever they met German resistance. In some places, even in small villages like Willersdorf, fighting was fierce with many casualties. The sweep missed us by only a few miles. However, all wooded areas and villages bordering the zone of operation were thoroughly searched for soldiers who had dressed in civilian clothes in order to evade capture. As the guns moved closer, our *Bürgermeister* issued instructions for us: "If troops enter Forchheim, we will announce their arrival by beating a drum. When you hear the drum, go immediately to the bunker under the restaurant. Stay inside. Stay out of the street."

The town's only public eating place was near my room, less than a block away. The owner, a nice lady, had been convinced for some time that the war's days were numbered, yet none of us knew what to expect. Americans, we were told, not Russians, would reach us first. Because some of my family had lived in America and had brought back good reports, I had high respect for Americans. But this was war.

I was alone with the children the afternoon the drum started, followed by the familiar scene of confused people running for shelter. I could hear shooting in the distance while the boys and I scurried to the bunker. We were inside for about an hour when the owner of the restaurant called down to us: "All right, you can come out now. Everything is okay."

We filed slowly out. I held a sleeping Norbert in my arms and Gunther and Kurt were on either side of me when I saw, for the first time in my life, an American, big and heavy-set. His eyes went back and forth over all of us and then came to rest on me. With his finger, he motioned that I should come to him. I was terrified. Despite assurances from the *Bürgermeister* that "Americans are gentlemen," I knew what often happened when conquering troops, bitter about war and tasting victory, took over enemy lands. I was certain this man was intent on some kind of harm–shoot me . . . or worse. I hesitated, my heart pounding. All around me people were crying, as visible proof of Germany's defeat, armed with machine guns, stood everywhere in the street. He began to advance toward me, hands outstretched, saying something in English.

"Don't be afraid of me" was the translation someone made. He put his hands on my shoulder. "Way over in America I have three little children like you have here." He smiled. Then, reaching into his pocket, he gave the boys some chewing gum and chocolate candy.

Greatly relieved, I was already back at the Haans when I heard some shooting. Almost immediately American soldiers pushed their way into my room and ordered us back to the bunker. They wanted my place for a lookout until they could determine where the shots were coming from. In my haste, I left everything behind, including my purse, which held Karl's gold watch and some other gold pieces.

Up to the last, no one, except maybe the lady who owned the restaurant, admitted loss of the war. No one said, "It's over." In fact, to his very last day, Hitler kept ordering the people to hold out, and even in remote villages like Willersdorf some rebels, angry about foreign troops on German soil, engaged the American military. Their stupid action got some people killed. When I finally got back to my quarters, the purse was there but the gold was gone.

The troops asked only for fresh milk and eggs and, after two or three days, withdrew from Willersdorf. What they left for us was a mound of bananas and a heap of burning K-rations. I never understood why they poured gasoline over a mountain of canned food when we were all so hungry, especially since they did not stop us from hunting through the smoldering pile and salvaging what we could. I picked up a banana and ate it, worms and all.

The end came on what was for us a quiet day in May, when American and Russian troops met each other in north-central Austria and all of Germany lay conquered. When the boys heard that the war had ended, their questions started again.

"Is Daddy coming soon? When will Daddy get here?" I still had no answer for them. We would pass the summer working outdoors, and hoping. I continued to write regularly to Karl and to Mrs. Czeipeck. No replies came.

One day, though, I did get a letter. It was from my sister's daughter Margaret, a registered nurse who had spent the war inside Germany. She was in Bamberg about fifteen miles to the north and, having located me through the Red Cross, wanted to live with me. I borrowed a bicycle, peddled to Bamberg, and returned with her and all her belongings, which fit handily into one knapsack. We were happy to be together and laughed merrily as we took turns riding each other through the countryside. She lost her nursing job when the war casualties stopped, but we both got work that summer crocheting big sun hats from reed-like grasses. Refugee labor was cheap, but we were paid in German marks and the busywork was fun.

We were also informed that refugee packages had arrived from the United States and that each family could have one. That package increased my purchasing power: I traded what I did not want for things I needed. For example, for one package of cigarettes I got a feather bed, and by bartering coffee, I got pillows and clothes for the children. I suppose this might be considered black market, but as far as I knew everybody did it and all parties seemed happy with their bargains. Then, too, the Haans gave me a share in the food. I remember my first bushel of wheat, which I promptly took to the mill, surrendering some of it as payment for having it ground. Yeast was not rationed, so I baked bread in the small oven in our room.

On another day I got a summons to the *Bürgermeister's* office. I had a pretty good idea what he would say because I had heard talk that it was safe for refugees to return to their own countries.

"Frau Gegner," he began, "you've been with us now for several months and have earned a good reputation in our community. But now that the war is over, I imagine you are very eager to go home to Yugoslavia. You can go now, for it is quite safe."

I could understand why Germany wanted to rid itself of refugees, but the inner voice which before had urged me to keep moving now said, "No! stay." I was still convinced that it was not safe for *Volksdeutsche* to return to Yugoslavia, and, besides, I had no intention of budging until I had some news of Karl. The Haans did not want me to leave either, because my labor was important for their harvest. So I stayed put; the boys and I were safe in Willersdorf.

Summer day faded into summer day. We watched the vegetables grow and the wheat mature. Kurt, Gunther, and even Norbert joined me in the fields, helping with the weeding and chopping of wood. When sugar beets were ready, I got all I wanted of them. The older boys knew all about sugar beets and did not complain for a moment when they got "fire duty." First, we gathered all kinds of dry firewood in the woods around the village. Then, one boy was in charge of keeping the outdoor fire burning and for days the "cook" continued. Each morning I filled a huge kettle with sugar beets, cooked them all day long, and in the evening strained the mushy pulp. The result was quarts and quarts of beet syrup–a perfect topping for the freshly-baked bread. My mother was right: "You never know when you'll need that."

Late summer meant slaughter time, and I was in for a backward glance in this enterprise too. There would be none of the clean, swift strokes my father had delivered. Instead, the event was a grotesque circus. The pigs were turned loose and the farmers chased them, swinging big axes. With every nip, the pigs let out a scream that made my skin crawl. Wildly, frantically they ran, with the farmers running after. When a pig was finally cornered, it was clubbed unconscious; then its head was cut off. I had never seen such cruel treatment of animals. After the carcasses were dressed, they were hung in an outside smokehouse and smoked until they were black. We saved every piece of fat, which was also completely black. These coal-like chunks served as lard. Everything cooked with either the meat or the fat turned black.

With the harvest completed, Kurt and Gunther returned to school. A year had now passed since the drums had boomed in Cservenka on the fateful morning when I had joined the thousands and thousands of displaced *Volksdeutsche*, displaced by a war begun by our ethnic relatives. Although the Haans and simple farmers like them seemed oblivious of the political philosophy of the Third Reich, the widespread attitude of Germans, as I would learn, became one of bitter, bitter skepticism. They were devastated about losing the war. Too many had believed Hitler's promises. For them, their betrayal was complete, their humiliation total. For most refugees, however, the let-down was hardly measurable; we already had lost our homes and most of our possessions.

Nuremburg, where I had spent one unforgettable night in a train station, was the place chosen for the war trials. Bit by bit, as unspeakable horrors of Nazism gradually came to view, I relived again some minor scenes from my own experience and was brought up short by the question I had earlier evaded putting into words: are the people to blame for the crimes of their leaders? I was like most Eastern Europeans who did not openly criticize decisions of the government. In the face of great evil–and I had seen some–is standing by and doing nothing ever excusable? Is it excusable when death is the sure and swift reward of action? I was not sure of the answer. Although I had known that Jews were being persecuted, I had not been aware of Hitler's obsession with a super race. What we had earlier scoffed at as preposterous–lampshades from Jewish skin– was actually true. I heard for the first time then about the concentration camps and the death camps with their gas chambers and crematoriums. We got a glimpse of Hell itself, and we heard that many Germans went crazy at the sight. Refugees spread the reports. The Germans I met shunned all talk.

Days were getting shorter and colder and my heart was heavy much of the time. As the months dragged by, I missed my husband more and more. I longed for the strength of his arms–around me, and to guide our sons. I needed someone to talk to, someone who had the answers to the moral questions, someone who would love me and take care of me, someone who could understand the searching of my soul. Not the Haans, not Margaret nor the boys could satisfy what I was looking for. Maybe Karl could.

I had started to pray with greater earnestness. Even though I did not know much about the God I was praying to, prayer brought me a strange calm. I did not then know the biblical teaching to "Humble yourselves, therefore, under the mighty hand of God, that He may exalt you at the proper time, casting all your anxiety upon Him, because He cares for you" (1 Peter 5:7). I sensed the firm hand but not the intimacy; I was kept steady, but I carried the full load.

Then a miracle happened: a note from Karl. It came in the mail, a small piece of dirty paper folded to look like an envelope and bearing a postal seal from Westphalia. Inside it read: "I'm alive, and I will be home soon." We all cried. People in the village rejoiced with us.

Westphalia. That meant Karl was near the Belgium border. Some Silesian refugees thought that *Volkssturm* from the Batschka were being held in a camp near Aachen. That was all I needed to know. Margaret thought she could manage the boys, so I dressed in the warmest clothing I had, which included Karl's leather jacket, walked through the forest to Forchheim and bought a train ticket with the money I had earned crocheting hats. The station was jammed with people and the train was already filled and pulling away.

"Wait! Wait!" I yelled, running with many others alongside the moving cars. Impulsively grabbing some hands extended from the windows, I was carried along until I finally got a foothold on a step and wiggled a place for myself. Bodies, like spiders, clung from open windows, doors, and passageways. Little by little we got rearranged, and men and boys let the women find places inside. For a day, a night, and part of another day the train moved across Germany, stopping at nearly every station. I had taken bread with me and occasionally we got water when the train stopped. The ride was miserable, but my hopes were high. "O please, God, let me find Karl."

The minute we reached Aachen, I jumped from the car and

began asking questions of attendants at the station.

"There was a camp here," said the man at the ticket window. "But it is deserted now. The prisoners have been moved."

"Where?" I cried, reaching for the counter to steady myself.

"I'm not sure, but I've heard Belgium."

I collapsed onto a nearby bench. With no papers to cross into Belgium, all I could do was return to Willersdorf, but I had to wait until morning for the next train. After eating some bread I felt stronger and walked around the city until I found a big dormitory where I could spend the night. To my surprise, I met many refugees looking for missing family members, several of them from the Batschka, though none from Cservenka. The man at the station was right; all prisoners had been taken to Belgium shortly before. Enveloped in a mood of pessimism and despair, we spent the evening and much of the night exchanging stories. Most, like me, had been wealthy. Now we wandered homeless in a foreign land with our husbands and sons prisoners of war. The uncertain future looked gloomy that night.

The train ride back was even worse: instead of hope my companion was discouragement. The boys read it on my face. "I didn't see Daddy," I told them. They could not understand why.

During the days which followed, I tried to hide my tears from the boys. But when the older two were in school, I often gave in to sessions of feeling sorry for myself. Once, when Norbert ran indoors from playing and would have caught me, I quickly lowered my head and buried my weepy face between my arms. Suddenly I felt baby arms around my neck.

"Daddy will come home soon," little Norbert whispered. "Everything will be all right."

* * * * *

Christmas 1945: our second Christmas as refugees. The entire village was scheduled to meet at the restaurant for a party, which included a program by the children. They all had pieces to recite telling of the birth of Jesus. Some spoke of the angel chorus, others of the shepherds, the wise men, and so forth. Then my boys had a turn.

"And what does Christmas mean to you, Kurt?" asked the narrator.

"It's Daddy's birthday!" he exclaimed, completely forgetting his lines. Everybody laughed. No one knew, of course, that it really was Karl's birthday, nor how tenaciously a young son had hoped his daddy would be home for Christmas.

. . . greater is He who is in you than
he who is in the world. (1 John 4:4b)

Chapter Ten

Strange Homecomings

Winter with its snow and wind kept us indoors most of the time. Even with the assurance that God was with me, I found it hard to stay optimistic about Karl. One muddy note in his handwriting–that was all I had to hang on to. He said he would be home soon. "How soon is soon?" I wondered.

With the melting of snow, the fields once more were soft for plowing. I looked forward to spending time outside but not to the heavy work. One cool afternoon as I trudged wearily behind the oxen, Frau Haan came running toward me with news that I had a letter from someone in Vienna. Immediately my thoughts jumped to the Czeipeck family. "At last!" I said to myself. "It must be from them or from the International Red Cross." To my surprise, the letter had nothing to do with Czeipecks. It was a note from a man from Cservenka who had been in the hospital with Georg when he died. For months he had been trying to trace me to see if I wanted Georg's personal effects. I wrote back asking for his papers. While leafing through them, I came upon a piece that looked familiar: a receipt for two horses and two wagons. They had passed the same checkpoint outside Vienna as we had! Poor Georg. I thought he might have been better off to have stayed in the hospital in Cservenka.

* * * * *

Spring plowing was not yet finished when one day I heard that Karl was on his way from the train station in Forchheim. People, some walking, some on bicycles, yelled to me as they passed by.

"We just saw your husband . . . he's coming through the woods! He's right behind us and will be here in a few minutes!"

From my place in the field I could see up ahead and there, coming out of the forests on the edge of Willersdorf, was what appeared to be an old man hobbling toward me and gripping the two sticks he used as canes. The sunlight reflecting from the top of his head indicated he was bald, and he looked little more than skin and bone.

"I wonder who that is," I said aloud while trying to steady the oxen. "He can hardly walk." I never would have guessed that *he* was Karl.

When he got close enough to recognize me—skinny body, wooden shoes and all—he cried out, "NO! my wife? Not my wife?" He ranted as if out of his mind and I was startled nearly out of my mine. What a homecoming. Apparently he still nurtured the image of a fine lady with servants, one he had provided with every material want. He had no idea what we had gone through—not only we but all refugees. Although I knew the wraith before me was indeed Karl, I had to fight a natural impulse to return a cry of my own: "No! not my husband!" Not only was he emaciated and without hair, but he had lost several teeth. My relief was mingled with disappointment. We tried to embrace, but Karl was so wobbly that I seemed to be hugging a skeleton. The pathetic scene got some relief when the boys, home from school, suddenly came running.

"Daddy, Daddy!" they cried, hanging on to his sleeves. I was afraid Karl might fall down, he was so weak.

"Gunther, Kurt," he said matter-of-factly, patting their heads. "You have grown. You are big boys now." We moved very slowly toward the house where Margaret was already standing outside with Norbert, who had been napping while I worked. Norbert hardly knew his daddy, and he approached very shyly to receive Karl's pat on the head. Gunther, meanwhile, being a sensitive boy, moved to the other side of me and quietly whispered, "Mamma, what's wrong with Daddy? Is he sick?" I nodded. If Kurt noticed anything strange, he kept it to himself.

Margaret had another place in Willersdorf to stay and left immediately, and although I had a husband again, it was in name only. Instead of a support and leader, I found myself with another dependent. I was anxious about Karl's physical health, a damage which would be remedied long before his mental stability returned. His bitter attitude was aggravated by the Haans, whom he looked down upon for being backward and uneducated and for speaking a German dialect he found hard to understand. I had gotten used to them, but unless I watched their mouths as they spoke, I still had a hard time understanding them. Karl would not try. He merely nodded his head to acknowledge their conversation, but he had little idea of what they were saying and he would not bother to find out. He thoroughly resented my working in the fields; that his wife was brought so low was a humiliation to him.

"But Karl," I would try to explain, "everybody has suffered. Actually, we have been better off than many because I have worked. The Haans and other farmers give us extra because they like me. Anyway, this is certainly no time to start putting on airs." Patiently I would coax him, and gradually I got him to accept that these conditions had been "normal" for quite some time. *Tante* Rettle regularly brought extra rations of food to him and he slowly gained strength. He was issued his own ration card and he also qualified to have his teeth fixed. Refugee relief furnished him with clothes.

Karl never volunteered any information, but I was curious about his experiences and began to ask him about the British prisoner of war camp.

"Did you have enough food?"

"No."

"Did they treat you right?"

"No."

"You mean they mistreated you?"

"Yes. Why do you keep asking? It hurts me too much to talk about it." But I persisted and he did admit that he had been beaten.

"Look!" he said sharply. "Germany isn't our country, yet I had to fight and I've lost everything—including my homeland. I don't want to talk about it . . . it's over."

"Yes, Karl," I put in, "it's over. But the Lord has been helping me, and He took care of you, too. We are alive, and we are together again. That's more than many people can say."

"How can God have let this happen?" Karl retorted, still bitter. "If Germany had won, maybe we could have gone home . . . but maybe not—there's still Tito." He was silent for several moments. "Kristina," he asked, his tone brighter, "how would you like to go to America?"

"America? So far? Way across the ocean?" America was

something people dreamed about, but dreams do not often come true.

"Yes, America. The United States. I'm going to write Uncle Ludwig right away. I lived with him and Aunt Louise near Seattle when I traveled years ago. Maybe they will agree to sponsor us." Karl had told me a little about Dr. Ludwig Heintz, a chiropractor, whose wife was Karl's father's sister. At Karl's mention of mail, however, I remembered the muddy note and showed it to him.

"How did you happen to mail this to me, and why didn't you write again?"

"You mean you got that?" He was amazed. "Before we were moved into Belgium, I found that piece of paper and scribbled on it. We were not allowed to send mail, but I looked for a chance. One day while I was working near a fence, a woman passed by. I threw it over and asked her to please mail it to my wife and children. I didn't really think she would."

"And I went all the way to Aachen to try to find you, but you were gone." I told him about my heartbreaking trip and what I had learned.

"I tried to smuggle a note out of Belgium too, but sending and receiving mail was forbidden. You mean no one notified you officially of my whereabouts? Poor Kristina. It must have been awful for you—not knowing if I were alive or dead."

At last Karl had spoken his concern for me. That was a healthy sign, and as he got stronger, he became increasingly dissatisfied with the current status of our lives and eagerly looked for opportunities to make life better for us.

Germany was divided among the conquerors: Britain, France, America, and Russia. We were fortunate to be in the American zone. Karl went to Hamburg and applied at headquarters there for a job as interpreter. Each day, about seven-thirty in the morning, the horn blowing would start at the end of the forest bordering Willersdorf. Up the main dirt street zoomed the Army jeep to pick up Karl. Every evening, when they brought him back, the driver again laid on the horn. This preferred treatment was a cause of tension and jealousy among the villagers, especially when the American soldiers gave our boys special goodies such as an orange, candy, and gum. The first time this happened, the boys, pleased with their present, quickly spread the word: "See! look what I got!" I told them that if they were not going to divide the orange or candy bar into as many pieces as there were refugee children, they better not go around bragging. Still, anything extra gave occasion for envy.

When Karl was strong enough, we began to walk to the Lutheran church. It had really been a blow to Karl the first time he heard the boys reciting what they had picked up during the times we worshipped with the Catholics. "I'll have no 'Hail Mary, mother of God' business in my house!" he exploded. "I'm grateful that Catholic families here were good to you and the boys," he added, "but I'll have no 'Hail Marys,' and that's final." That was final.

Although Norbert had developed a cough, things were going along rather nicely for us. We had enough to eat and packages continued to arrive, not only for general refugee relief, but also items from family in the United States. Karl was respected by the Americans and his mental outlook and physical health improved steadily. My working in the fields did not seem to bother Karl quite as much when he did not have to watch me. Also, it boosted his morale when his aunt and uncle guaranteed to help us settle in Seattle.

Refugees by the millions had poured into Germany during the final days of the war and immediately after, and the problems relating to our resettlement were monumental. My niece Margaret, through her connections with the Red Cross, had located a few family members; she also found out that many people from Yugoslavia, including the Batschka and Banat, had congregated in Munich. Eager to learn what we could, Karl and I left the boys with Margaret and took the train. We located a compound for refugees on the outskirts of the city where many of them were staying. Although refugees might be reluctant to reveal personal indignities against themselves, they seldom withheld what they knew about others. We were shocked at what we heard. All the people we met were crying, some uncontrollably, as, one after the other, these *Volksdeutsche* relived horrors they had been part of. We talked first with refugees from our own town of Cservenka.

"A few days after you left, the Russians and the Partisans came," began one of the women. "They put us in the Hotel Stock right down the street from you . . . you know the place. They just took over our homes, everything . . . and rounded us up and drove us like cattle. Many were robbed of even the clothes on their backs. Some who put up a fight were killed. I saw . . . "

She choked, unable for a time to go on and the others, apparently jolted back in time and place and seeing again their particular nightmares, were silent. So totally did they seem to identify with the speaker that no one broke in to rescue her. When at length she collected herself, she haltingly explained about the death camps.

"Many old people and people who were sick and children too young to make good workers were killed . . . shot or left to starve. They showed no compassion, not for anybody." She stopped speaking and stared ahead blankly.

"Your house is not the same," said a former neighbor who had delayed leaving until it was too late. "All the trees, even the fence, were cut down for firewood. Whenever we were marched past your house on the way to work," she continued, "I saw smoke coming from windows and from the hole cut in the roof. And when I got a chance to look inside—you're not going to believe this—there was a fire burning with a big, black kettle hanging above it. And this was right in the middle of your beautiful living room!"

"Russians did that?" I blurted out.

"No, not Russians. After the Red Army sent some of the young people off to Russia, they didn't stay around very long. It was Tito's Partisans. Some of them were so primitive that they didn't know how to live in a modern house. Others were just bandits—they plundered everything. Many were brutal . . . I was lucky . . . I didn't get raped. All people I knew about were forced out of their homes."

"Then after we were in the Hotel Stock for a few months, we were moved to a big farm. You know the place—old Peter Vetter's farm." A woman I was not acquainted with had picked up the story. "From there we had to march to the work projects. Many dropped dead every day because we were on near-starvation diets."

"And it was doubly terrible when someone in your own family died," interjected another. "Then you would have to stay with the body until the wagon came around, and then you had to pick the body up yourself and place it on top of whatever corpses were already there. When the cart was full, the dead were dumped into a common grave . . . and relatives had to dig it, too. Crying and so weak they could barely stand up . . . it was awful."

The room grew still again for a few moments. Apparently no one had missed being an eyewitness to this treatment of the dead. I did not know what Karl was thinking, but his jaw was set in anger. As people and places were named, I focused them in my mind and scanned the long-familiar scenes. Our town's popular hotel–I had often attended social gatherings with Karl in the big, fancy ballroom with its red velvet draperies and polished floors. . . . A more recent vision–that of buildings crammed full of refugees lying on filthy, lice-infested straw–came into view. Refugee camps, though, even with squalid conditions, are not concentration camps; refugees are not prisoners. . . . The Vetter brothers owned several big grain farms in Cservenka, and they used to bring their grain to the Gegner and Feldman silos. So, one of their wealthy estates had also been converted. . . . "Rounded up and marched like cattle . . ." Now it had happened to other neighbors, Gentiles this time. *Mein Gott, das kann doch nicht sein!*" (My God, it just can't be!)

The moan escaped my lips, but I did not further voice the agony I was feeling. I was young; I was strong; I was a woman; I was rich; I was German and I had three children, the oldest only nine, barely old enough to count when it came to a work crew. All the evils visited on Cservenka would have found me. The perverse wind had continued to blow there. . . .

"Did any of the ones who left in the evacuation return?" The question was Karl's.

"I did," came a raspy whisper from a man of about sixty. "But there was nothing to come back to except the hunger camp. I never should have believed the propaganda that we could return home." He paused for a time, and when no one else spoke, he continued. "And another thing . . . and this is kind of funny when you think about it. Remember how we all dug up our yards to hide our valuables for the few days we'd be gone? Well, a lot of that stuff was carried off by the Russians. But what is funnier is that some people, including me, took along only their oldest clothes so they wouldn't get their nice things dirty. We expected to find everything just as we left it, even clothes hanging neatly in the closets. I've asked myself over and over, 'How stupid can you be?' But right now I'm thankful to be alive. My second escape was far worse than the first, but I'd risk everything to get out of Cservenka. Several of us sneaked our way into Austria. We had to cross mined fields, and not all of us made it."

My thoughts jumped to Sophia and Josef and panic surfaced again. They had insisted on returning. They were convinced all was safe. The Banat where they lived was east of Cservenka. It would be just as bad, maybe even worse, there. From what all these people had seen in Cservenka, they all agreed: *Volksdeutsche* were being erased from Yugoslavia. Anyone with a German-sounding name, even some Serbs who did not speak German, had been rounded up.

Karl and I were emotionally drained by these reports, so dazed, in fact, that I could hardly walk around the compound. Later that day, we found some who had survived Silesia and Czechoslovakia. I froze as I listened.

Many from the wagon train which left from Cservenka, including those in Karl's family that I had traveled with before I joined my own sister, had been directed to Silesia when Vienna got overcrowded. "No woman was safe from the Russian soldiers, not even an eighty-five year old." The one telling the story knew that Kati and Martha had been in Silesia. She told how mothers would hide their teenage daughters in hay piles. "Troops made rounds in the middle of the night," she explained. "That was their main entertainment. They were vicious. Sometimes five of them would take the same girl and at gunpoint force other family members to watch. Some girls died; some went crazy."

"Not Kati and Martha! O Karl! I would have been there too if Sophia and Josef had not caught up with me. But it wasn't that bad in Czechoslovakia, was it?" I asked, directing my attention back to our informants. "What about the *Volksdeutsche* in Pilzen? When I left, they were certain they would be safe. The area wasn't being bombed."

"In some sense, that was worse yet," volunteered two sisters who had made it to safety. "In that camp, not Russians but Poles and Czechs tried to outdo each other in getting even with Germany. The refugees killed outright were the lucky ones." They then told how they had been left to starve, deprived of all food, even water; and as their desperation increased, with their fingers they would go after any root they could pry from the ground. "What some found was poisonous," said one, "and they died agonizing deaths. We're lucky to be alive."

"You were smart to leave when you did," said the other, smiling faintly.

So the hate that had sent chills through me at the food tables had indeed vented itself!

I still had one more concern, about Vienna and the Czeipecks. My letters did not come back, but I never got an answer and Margaret had not been able to get information on them through the Red Cross. Karl and I asked around and found some in the group who recently had been in Vienna. They said the city had been bombed more than fifty times and that the Opera House and the area around it had been hit. I felt sick. That is where the Czeipeck home was located.

The information coming at me was overwhelming. I could not assimilate all of it at once. Although we spent a couple days in the camp, it was not until our return trip that I tried to put words to my thoughts. I wanted Karl to know about the choices I had faced after he left our wagon train in Hungary. I now knew where the alternatives to my decisions had led.

"Karl," I began hesitantly after we had ridden for about half an hour, "you heard all those stories. I could have been in any one of those places. I could have ended up in Silesia with Kati and Martha . . . I could have stayed in Vienna with the Czeipecks . . . I could have stayed in Czechoslovakia. I might even have tried to return home, either on my own or with Sophia and Josef–they wanted me to go with them and we still don't know where they are. But always . . . always . . ."

"Yes? Go on, Kristina. What is it?"

"But always, an inner voice . . . or something . . . gave me directions. And except when I first decided to go with Sophia, people actually thought I was crazy. And I admit my actions did not always seem reasonable. But I was urged to keep moving–'Keep going, keep going,' a voice seemed to say. And it seems now that I was not foolish after all. In every case, the boys and I were better off. You heard for yourself what people went through. Karl, that can't be just coincidence. I know the Lord was telling me what to do. I never could have done what I did on my own initiative! I'm just not like that!"

Karl stared straight ahead, a grave expression on his face. He said nothing. After several minutes, he took my hand in his, and, still without turning, he slowly and deliberately began to nod his head. We rode most of the way in silence. What we had learned in Munich was having its astounding impact.

* * * * *

After we had been back in Willersdorf for several weeks, Margaret got word that Sophia, Josef, and Ibi were in Karlsruhe, Germany. They had not been able to cross into Yugoslavia. After what we had learned about the hunger camps there, that was good news. They spent months in a refugee camp in southern Hungary in extremely poor conditions, and although they suffered more than I did, they fared better than those in Silesia and Czechoslovakia. Kati, Jani, and Martha (all having been mistreated) settled eventually near Hanover in Germany. Diel Baschti must have gotten separated from them somewhere and we never learned his whereabouts. Besides Johan and Georg, Karl lost another brother, Willie, and I lost my brother Josef, whose widow died of grief. Both of them were in the *Volkssturm*; they never came back and were presumed dead. All other members of both sides of the family (including Karl's stepmother) had gotten out of Yugoslavia, never to live there again.

* * * * *

Christmas 1946 would be special because our family was together. We would yet face distress in Germany, but that knowledge was hid from us. Karl would not attend the Catholic church on Christmas Eve and it was too dark and cold to walk to the next village, so we stayed in our room while I baked a very simple cake for Karl's birthday the next day. When I had finished and we were sitting quietly together, Karl handed me, rather shyly I thought, a wartime *Feldpostkarte* (military postcard) with something in his own handwriting.

"Here, Kristina. This is for you."

As I read the poetic lines written in pencil on the piece of flimsy war-grade paper, my eyes glistened. Karl, too, was holding to what was precious.

FLANDERISCHE WEIHNACHT 1945

(CHRISTMAS 1945 IN FLANDERS)

The old ancient hymns and a few little lights
Was all that we had on that holiest of nights!
The holiest of nights found us relentlessly chained
In Flanders, in Belgium, while war status reigned.

Yet never have eyes been so burning ablaze,
Yet never have faces looked paler those days,
Yet never before did the spark from a wick
Sink deeper in hearts which with longing were sick.
This Christmas is safe from the hands of a thief,
This Christmas is sacred to our belief.
We firmly believe in the Way and the Light,
And that some day this darkness forever subside.
And shall we encounter each other some other day,
Outside of this camp, in an era less gray,
Then we will know it, yet no one will say:
"The old ancient hymns and a few little lights
Was all that we had on the holiest of nights."
This Christmas gave everything to us in prison:
It gave us the strength of the Christ born and risen.

> [Translation from the German is by
> Beate Peter]

Let us hold fast the confession of our hope without wavering,
for He who promised in faithful. (Hebrews 10::20)
The LORD is good, a stronghold in the day of trouble,
And He knows those who take refuge in Him. (Nahum 1:7)

Chapter Eleven

The Long Wait

In time the Americans withdrew from Bamberg and Karl lost his job as interpreter. While looking for other work, he read in the paper that construction workers were needed to rebuild Freiburg, a resort city of the Black Forest near the French border. Karl went on ahead to look for a place to live, and the boys and I followed in a truck, having received a ride with other refugees traveling from Willersdorf to Freiburg. We found a disappointed Karl.

"Bad news," he said. "The only housing in this city is this place," he explained, pointing to the building behind him. "And it is for construction workers only, not for their families. Freiburg is a mess."

"Then what will we do?" I blurted out, fearing we had run into another closed door. "We can't sleep in the street. They have to let us stay with you."

"I'm afraid not; I already checked. But let's walk around. Lots of places are deserted. Maybe we can find something which will at least get us out of the weather. And Kristina," he added, putting his arm around my shoulder, "I'll be staying with you and the boys."

As we walked together along the streets of Freiburg, I saw how right Karl was. Much of the city was in shambles. At last we came to what at one time had been a solid, brick compound, apparently administrative headquarters for the military. Some walls were standing, but the roof and top floor were gone and all windows and doors were blown out. Debris lay everywhere, inside and out.

"Well, what do you think, Kristina?" Karl looked at me quizzically.

"It seems I didn't have to worry about doors being slammed in our faces after all! This place doesn't have any." I grinned in spite of myself.

We all pitched in and cleaned up, and that night, sleeping on the floor on the few clothes we had, we shared one small room with bedbugs and an occasional rat.

The next day, Karl and the boys hunted through the rubble for pieces of wood to board up windows and to make a door. The task proved gruesome. Karl went immediately to the authorities, who then made a thorough search of the building and dug up the yard. The war had been over for more than two years, and still there were some dead soldiers and parts of bodies under these ruins!

In the weeks that followed, Karl made a makeshift table and some chairs from scraps of wood. Fortunately, I had been able to bring along my small stove, so we had heat and I could cook. There was no flue, so we piped the smoke out through the wall, which worked quite well except when wind currents hit head-on. Then the choking smoke billowed back into the room.

We had been in Freiburg but a few days when Pastor Kiefer, a small, white-haired man who reminded me of Pastor Keck from my confirmation days, came to call. Someone had told him about a needy family. Through his Lutheran congregation, we got a bed, some cooking gear, and some used clothes. I got busy and ripped up some woolen goods that did not fit and reknitted the yarn into socks, sweaters, and gloves for the children. When I was finished, there were scraps left over of several different colors, enough to make a single glove for me. I did not want to waste a thing, and neither did other people, so multi-colored, homemade clothes were "in style," and one glove was better than nothing. I always kept the other hand in my pocket and because I thought nothing about it, I was surprised when, one Sunday after church services, a lady in the congregation politely inquired what happened to my other glove. When I explained how it came to be one of a kind, we both had a good laugh. As I walked away, however, my eyes got misty: the woman had really cared about me, a refugee. From this congregation, we were also given a Bible, which we read at mealtime and before bed.

That spring, Gunther was confirmed. For his special verse, he memorized a portion from the Psalms:

> Search me, O God, and know my heart;
> Try me and know my anxious thoughts;
> And see if there be any hurtful way in me,
> And lead me in the everlasting way.
> (Psalm 139:23-24)

Hearing his recitation before the congregation, I thought back to my own confirmation and was amazed at how God had used circumstances of the war to bring me to the place of admitting how far I had wandered from the text I had chosen as a guide for my life:

> Take my instruction, and not silver,
> And knowledge rather than choicest gold.
> For wisdom is better than jewels;
> And all desirable things cannot compare with her.
> (Proverbs 8:10-11)

I had neither honored God with my wealth nor had I bothered about wisdom. For years I had been satisfied with silver, gold, and jewels, and now they were gone. But God was not gone.

Karl's job meanwhile was very hard physical labor carrying coal to the homes of the French who occupied this section of Germany. To them we were still the hated enemy, and all workers were treated as slave laborers. Yet I never heard Karl complain about the hard work, only that his pay was not enough to feed us. So when I learned of a training course in baby nursing which I could take, I enrolled and later received a license as a baby nurse. My first job was with a French family.

The woman was not sick after her delivery, but she stayed in bed most of the time. I suspected that many French people had been very poor in France, yet here in Germany her family and others like them took over the best rooms in German homes or forced the Germans completely out as they moved in. She was extremely rude to me and one time when I pricked my own finger while pinning a diaper, thus getting a drop of blood on the cloth, she accused me of deliberately sticking her baby and made a terrible fuss. The people at the German agency laughed about the silly episode, but they got me another job. My working helped financially, but it also meant that Norbert was left alone until Gunther and Kurt got home from school.

Our first winter in Freiburg was cold and rainy, and one night, while all of us like five herrings were lying in our one bed, I heard some drips. The water started down toward us, one floor at a time. So in the middle of the night we all picked our way carefully and climbed the three damaged flights to the roof and shoveled the water off with scraps of wood. But we had not remedied the problem—only a new roof could do that. The little room where we slept, cooked, washed, and ate was therefore very damp and we had very little light from outdoors because we did not have glass to replace broken windows and had to board them all up.

Our second winter, Norbert got almost deathly ill with asthma. He was put into a hospital where for months doctors tried one drug after another, one test after another, but with no success. Then Gunther had a relapse with his lungs, and we put him in a sanatorium. Gunther recovered and was able to go back to school, but Norbert seemed to get sicker. Yet no treatment helped and he always cried when we left him. After one visit, while Karl and I were going down the stairs from the fourth floor of the sanatorium, we heard "Mommy, Mommy, please take me home!" I looked at my husband, he looked at me, and we ran upstairs, grabbed Norbert and carried him out. He was home with us again, but that meant I had to stop working and our meager funds dwindled to nothing.

The day arrived when we did not know where the next meal would come from. While I washed clothes on a washing board in the kerosene-lit room, listening to the drips of rain as they hit the old dishes placed here and there to catch them, desperate and with tears rolling down my face, I took action: I prayed. Then I waited. I was alone with Norbert, who was in bed where he stayed all the time because he was too ill to walk. When the knock came, I lifted the inside latch on the homemade door and gazed at the stout woman carrying a large basket.

"Who sent you?" I asked, although to myself I fully acknowledged her as from the Lord.

"Are you Frau Gegner? Pastor Kiefer sent me. I'm from the church. When we heard about you and your husband and three children living so poorly in this place, members donated this food and today I thought to bring it to you." The basket held food enough for several days.

Through my tears I could hardly find a word to say. I know that Karl was thankful too. Although he was a proud man who believed in earning his own way, I saw in his manner how genuinely grateful he was for this demonstration of charitable concern. He was a man of few words, but he felt deeply. We were growing closer in our marriage, and our family, despite illness and hardship, was looking hopefully to the future. We had made a formal request to immigrate to the United States; Karl would soon get a better job restoring buildings instead of carrying heavy coal; we would better our living conditions; Gunther's tuberculosis would be pronounced cured; and the cause of Norbert's severe asthma would be diagnosed and successfully treated. I traced our uplifting in large part to the kind gesture of having our need for food met on the very day we reached the bottom–not before and not a day later. My trust in God continued slowly to grow and I began to recall promises I had learned in my childhood, such as: ". . . for the LORD your God is the one who goes with you. He will not fail you or forsake you" (Deut. 31:6). Even though I had forsaken and failed Him, the Lord had nevertheless been faithful to His word and had been with me. And He would provide this Scripture again in circumstances which would test my faith–for faith, like a muscle, grows stronger only as it is tried.

As months passed and we little by little explored our building, we discovered that one of the back rooms was a kitchen and that there was another room opening from it that could be used as a bedroom. Both rooms were filthy, but as we began to clean, we saw that the kitchen had a good tile floor, which I, of course, scrubbed and scrubbed and waxed until it looked like new. Whenever we had visitors, in order to reach our rooms they had to walk down a long corridor of badly damaged flooring and broken-out walls. As they would step through our doorway and suddenly come upon a gleaming floor, their exclamations always pleased me. If nothing else, I once more had a polished floor! On his construction job, Karl managed to get some glass and fixed a window, giving us daylight. Here, we were also able to vent fumes from our stove through a hole in the ceiling and were no longer bothered by smoke.

In 1948 we got our first application form for immigration to the United States. Some of the questions dealt with military duty. In the final months of the war, Karl and all Yugoslavian Germans he knew had been designated SS. Yet Karl never did fight. In fact, he never wore a German uniform or carried a weapon. The uniform he wore when he was with us in Hungary was Yugoslavian. Nevertheless, in the soft flesh of his inside left arm, he bore the tattooed seal that he belonged to Hitler, and he had received harsh treatment as a prisoner of war because of it, all of which added to his bitterness. From what we heard after the war about the activities of the SS, I was frantic that we would not be allowed to enter the United States even though Karl had not volunteered for service and had been drafted against his will.

"We've got to get rid of that mark," I exclaimed to Karl after reading the application form.

"I once asked a doctor about removing it," Karl said, "and he mentioned a medication that's supposed to take care of it. I'll try to get some."

The next day, we locked ourselves in a room away from the children and I went to work. "Be careful," Karl warned. "It's supposed to be powerful stuff."

"Good. Maybe if I rub and rub, I can get the letters off. Then the skin will heal as good as new." I began the rubdown. It must have hurt terribly because in short time I had passed completely through the skin and into raw flesh, but Karl humored me and did not complain for quite a while.

"I think this is enough," he said, finally. "I think you are almost to the bone!"

One day went by, then two days, and on the third day Karl's sore arm was so red and infected that we had to go to the doctor.

"One more day," the doctor exclaimed, "and your husband could have lost his arm." With blood poisoning already well on its way, Karl was immediately hospitalized. Karl had been thoroughly screened both at the time of his release from prison camp and when he worked for the Americans in Bamberg, so his mark did not later interfere with our immigration, but my forcing what was intended to be a gradual process could have cost Karl an arm and maybe even his life.

We took our time filling out the forms, keeping an identical copy for ourselves. That was a good thing, because every three or four weeks for nearly four years, we got the same forms to fill out again. In all, we filled them out about forty times. The annoying procedure was a test to trip up anyone who might be lying. Although they were aware of Karl's SS brand, the officials never probed on this point. We concluded they were easier on Karl than on younger men because they knew Hitler's call for the *Volkssturm* had come late in the war and that most older men and young boys had not willingly joined with Germany. Furthermore, that he had been allowed to work for the Americans in Bamberg clearly confirmed that Karl was not a Nazi sympathizer. We heard that men in their twenties and thirties had it much tougher, however, and that many were denied immigration to the United States, Canada, and South America.

* * * * *

"Kristina," Karl said one day, "I know it's hard for you to have to stay inside all the time with Norbert. He can't walk and he doesn't eat much. He's eight years old and he's been in school only a few weeks. He seems to be going backwards in his development." I agreed, but I did not know what we could do about it. We had tried everything.

"On my job I've learned about a military doctor who specializes in asthma, and with very good results. Maybe we should try again."

We carried Norbert to the hospital a few blocks away.

"I want you to bring the child here every day for a week," the doctor said after examining Norbert, "and I will inject him."

When I heard "inject," I bristled. "No, doctor. He's been injected so many times that you can see marks all over his body. He'll have no more injections. My child is not a guinea pig."

"Frau Gegner," he said, looking me straight in the eye, "I guarantee you, after one week your boy is going to get better." His manner convinced us.

I followed the orders and the doctor was right. Like leprous Naaman in the Bible, who, according to the word of Elisha the prophet, was not cured of his disease until he had dipped himself in the river seven times,[4] so it happen with Norbert. His injections this time were not shots but intravenous drippings into his arm and for six days he did not seem to improve: I still had to carry him to and from the hospital. But on the seventh day, Norbert walked. He even climbed the stairs. And when we got home, he began to ask for food and there seemed to be no end to his appetite. He gained weight and steadily improved. The change was miraculous, and we thanked the Lord. At last he could go to school, and we purged ourselves of everything with fur—the cause of his allergy.

We were always glad to get packages from the United States containing clothes, but as Norbert got well, we noticed that nothing was small enough for him. Once, he grabbed a pair of trousers about

Gunther's size and, holding them up with both hands, pranced around the room shouting, "Look Mamma! They fit!" Actually two Norberts could have fit inside.

In the fall of 1950, the turn came for our building to be restored. Pastor Kiefer had tried to get us a flat long before, but not until we were forced out by construction workers were we able to move into an apartment. Although small—two bedrooms plus bath—the place was new and totally without bedbugs. For the first time in years, I did not have to fight biting pests.

With our change in housing came a change to a Lutheran congregation closer to us and a completely different style of preaching. Pastor Kiefer had focused on Christian deeds done from a loving heart; Pastor Zitt called us to repentance and faith. In Germany, most Germans I met said they had lost their faith when they were betrayed by Hitler. Not many people went to church, and only a handful attended each Sunday where we went. So the plea for repentance was in order, but his tactics seemed extreme. For instance, in sermon after sermon he painted horrible pictures of how bad the Russians were and said they were preparing for war, this time using insects and bacterial warfare. Such messages from a pulpit were a new experience for me; I was accustomed to a softer approach. The man was obviously deeply stirred and spoke from apparent conviction, but I was disturbed by his fists pounding "Repent! Repent! Repent!" The war had not been my fault; what did I have to repent of? I often left church unsettled.

In the spring of 1951, Kurt was confirmed by Pastor Zitt. Like Gunther, for his special Scripture he picked a verse in the Psalms:

> I will instruct you and teach you in the way you
> should go;
> I will counsel you with My eye upon you.
> (Psalm 32:8)

The rest of 1951 came and went. With each application form and each letter and Care Package from relatives in the United States, the more eager we grew to be on our way. For a long time the boys and I had been studying English, thinking we would know the language by the time we reached American shores. Karl was fluent in English, but he lacked the patience to teach us more than a word now and then.

"What's this?" I asked, sifting through our latest Care Package.

"What is 'Jello,' and how do I fix it."

"All I remember is that you put the Jello in hot water," he answered. "That's all I know about it." Sticky, sweet water did not seem much of a treat to me. We did not know what peanut butter was either. We understood the word "butter," but with our first taste, all of us made a face. This was not butter. Packaged, dry soup was another new item. We were getting prepared for life in the United States.

Then came the request for us to report for physical examinations. One at a time we had to take a turn standing naked before a team of doctors. How relieved and thankful I was that all of us were then well and that Karl had had his hernia repaired–an injury he got hauling coal. Immigration was so strict at the time that anyone with, for example, varicose veins did not pass the test.

We all passed and shortly thereafter were notified that our visas were ready. What a day! Grabbing and hugging each other, we laughed and cried, over and over again. Our orders were to report to a camp at Hanover and from there to a ship.

Winter, 1952: seven and a half years since I had fled my Yugoslavian homeland. Now I would begin life anew in a land whose language and customs were foreign to me. The lush grass many of us *Volksdeutsche* had dreamed of finding in the land of our ancient kin turned out to be stubble. We had lived in a far country too long. All *Volksdeutsche*, Hitler had insisted, owed their allegiance, even their blood, to the *Vaterland*. Yet those from Yugoslavia, and possibly from other countries as well, often were not acknowledged as being true Germans. I, for one, wanted to get out of Germany. Karl felt the same way.

After such a long wait, our actual exodus took place quickly. There would be no fanfare. We returned the furniture and other household items lent to us and said our goodbyes to our friends. Then we were put on a train for Hanover, where we would stay one week in barracks before proceeding to the North Sea port at Bremerhaven. Except for a brief overnight visit with Karl's sister Kati and her family who lived near Hanover, there was no family to see us off. We were, after all, only *Fluschtligen* (refugees); we were only passing through. Our refuge was yet another far country.

* * * * *

I could end my story here: our family had survived the war; we were all healthy and together; and we had the happy prospect of going to a new land and beginning a new life. Although I had lost everything connected with my former life—riches, status, home and homeland—I was already recognizing that I had actually gained, because in being brought low I had found God. While I was fleeing along an uncertain path, He protected and guided me. In earlier years, He had blessed me with plenty, but I, foolishly thinking I was in control of my life, had been too proud to give Him the credit.

The final months of the war and the seven years following had gradually showed me how little control I actually had, yet even then I had not asked God to prepare my way. I had sometimes called out to Him, but my cry was not so much from faith as from fear. I now believe God was answering the prayers of someone else on my behalf, and the only person I know of who consistently prayed for me and for my salvation was my mother. But in order for the Lord to answer her prayers for me, I had to be brought to a place where He could get my attention, because God does not force anyone to obey Him. God had my attention, but I knew very little about Him. I had been baptized and confirmed Lutheran without fully knowing God as He revealed Himself in Jesus, because in those years I had not really been listening. I had tried to keep the Ten Commandments and had lived a moral life. When that had not satisfied me, I turned to material wealth to fill my need. That worked for a while only because I avoided thinking about God. I squeezed Him out and had lived in my fairy tale world until I was thrown suddenly into the miseries of war. There God met me. I was thankful for His protection and for the peace He had given me in the course of my wanderings, but I did not praise Him. Something was still missing.

The faith I had in Europe, though genuine, was not mature. God had proved His faithfulness: by directing me from one refugee camp to another and by sending food when we had no means to buy it. After I clearly saw His providence, trust came fairly easy. My war experiences showed me God as benefactor, and my faith rested on that. Would it hold when, like Job, I would have the props knocked out from under me?

In 1952, my political haven in the United States was guaranteed. My spiritual refuge, however, was yet to be confirmed.

*"Peace I leave with you; My peace I give to you; not
as the world gives, do I give to you. Let not your
heart be troubled, nor let it be fearful." (John 14:27)*

Chapter Twelve

New Life

"Is that our ship?" cried three very excited boys as they pointed
to the end of the pier where the old military vessel was tied.

"That's it!" replied an equally excited Karl. "I've heard it's having
this last run before being scrapped."

More than a thousand refugees, all *Volksdeutsche* from Yugoslavia,
Rumania, and Bulgaria, were gathering on the huge pier waiting to
board. During the forty-eight hours we stayed in barracks at
Bremerhaven, we talked with families who had stories similar to ours.
All had fled their homes nearly eight years earlier, wandering from
place to place, often without food and often in great fear for their
lives. In many cases, families would never be united again. But on this
blustery February morning, cheeks were red and eyes sparkled; a new
life lay ahead.

When our turn came, carrying cardboard boxes which held a
change or two of clothes received earlier from relatives in the United
States, we climbed the gangplank. At the top, men and women were
separated. Because Norbert was almost ten years old, even he had to
be with his father, and I was all by myself with other women and girls
in the front of the ship–the worst place to be. In the cubby holes
called rooms, the bunks were so low and close together that moving
around was impossible.

The actual crossing was typical for the Atlantic in winter. For
eleven days I never got away from the pitching of the ship nor the
constant chugging of the motor. I was seasick the entire time, but I
had lots of company on that score. Karl, who served as an

interpreter, kept urging me to walk on deck, but the wind and rain were icy cold and waves were mountainous, especially when the ship passed through the Bay of Biscay off France.

Karl and the boys, however, felt great. For years they had been hungry for good food, and it seemed they could not get filled up. They had meat, eggs, milk, butter, and all the fruits they wanted. Their shrunken stomachs stretched quickly. Gunther, now sixteen, worked in the kitchen, so he got first choice on food. That the boys were eating well was for me the only bright spot on the trip, the only bright spot, that is, until the shouts started.

"We're almost there! Come, look! We're almost there! See! That's the Statue of Liberty!"

Almost everyone scrambled to a deck. The sea was calm and sickness was forgotten. Even though the March day was cold and hazy, the shipful of refugees stayed on deck, totally captivated by the towering symbol of liberty.

At Ellis Island we went through customs. The place was confusion as the officers ripped open "suitcases," by now dilapidated. The experience was utterly frustrating because I could not understand a word being spoken, other than Yes and No. Getting a new language was not going to be as easy as I had thought.

As soon as we passed through customs, we were greeted by my sister Sophia, who had immigrated three years earlier, and Karl's cousin, neither of whom at that time had enough money to sponsor us. During our two-day visit, I got my initiation into American luxury.

"But I didn't!" Sophia replied when I exclaimed that she should not have planned such an elaborate breakfast for us. "We have this every morning–grapefruit, eggs and toast, pancakes with syrup. This is how most people start the day."

"It just can't be," I thought, "that average people live so well."

Soon we were on our way to Chicago, where we saw Karl's stepmother and her daughter, Hilda, who had been in the States for one year. Next, we again got on the train, this time for our final destination, the Pacific Northwest. The vastness of our new homeland overwhelmed me as did sights such as the faces of four presidents carved into Mt. Rushmore and the magnificent peaks of the Rocky Mountains.

After three days and nights, we pulled into the station at

Edmonds, Washington, slightly north of Seattle, and were met by our sponsors, Louise and Ludwig Heintz, Karl's aunt and uncle. They had advanced our fare from New York and had gotten a job for Karl doing grounds maintenance for a school district. Compared to the coal carrying he had done for almost no pay in Europe, to garden for a living wage was quite agreeable. After putting us up for six weeks, the Heintzes made a generous proposal: they would buy us a house and we would pay them back according to the going rates at the banks. So in May, we had our first home, on Corliss Avenue in north Seattle. We immediately enrolled the boys in school, and I began a new phase of adjustment.

I was no longer a refugee–I had a country; yet I felt a growing isolation because I did not have the language of the people. Although I had some relief on Sundays when we attended a German Lutheran church, during the week it was quite different. For instance, when I was out in the yard working and a neighbor would greet me in English, I felt foolish with my "me Germany." In a short time, I could not even understand my own family. The boys had new expressions every day and wanted to practice with Karl, so I was left out and they did not want to slow down for me.

"Well," I thought, "I'll show you. I'm going to read the paper every day even if I don't understand it. If I read every day, I'll be able to speak." That delusion did not last long. I grew increasingly hungry for the German language, and although most neighbors were friendly and tried to help me, we heard reports that at least one neighbor had said, "We don't need any Hitlers in our neighborhood."

"Here too?" I cried. "Are we going to get the same treatment here as we did in Europe?" Much later, when I could speak English, I went to the family and told our story. In time we became close friends, but it bothered me that he generalized, putting all German people into one category.

Before long Gunther, Kurt, and Norbert wanted to attend an American church where they could associate with younger people. We therefore joined the Ravenna Boulevard Presbyterian congregation where Pastor Sidney Hammond worked with an especially friendly youth group. Our boys took active parts right away. And there was a bonus for me, too: I met the Webber sisters, whose parents were *Volksdeutsche* from Russia, so I still had opportunity to speak German.

Karl and the boys all had jobs, but with my language barrier, there was little I could do to bolster the family income except domestic cleaning and fruit picking. Our second summer in Seattle, I went therefore with the boys to a cherry orchard on the other side of Lake Washington. One day, while I was up a tree, a very pregnant young woman stood beneath me. I had spied her earlier buying cherries from the owner. She motioned for me to get down, and, working through Gunther as an interpreter, I learned she was offering me a job: help her with housework until her baby was born, and then take care of the newborn. Of course I accepted, and while she wrote directions for me to get to her house by bus, I laughed to myself. Mrs. Johannsen had not known I was a trained baby nurse, but the Lord knew. It was through the recommendation of this kind Norwegian woman that I would finally get the other help I needed. The next new mother that I took care of was an English teacher! From then on, with further recommendations, I got steady baby care jobs, which I still do occasionally, second generation in many cases. With all of us working, we gradually made inroads into our debt to Uncle Heintz and also for about fifty dollars we bought an old, old Packard—our first car.

In other ways, too, life in America took some getting used to. For example, that first summer of 1952 was a presidential election campaign. One evening as we watched Eisenhower give a speech on a neighbor's television, the neighbor pointed to the screen and shouted, "Do you really mean that?"

"Of course he means it," I said in my broken English. "How can you question what a president says?" In Europe, we were taught to believe whatever the government said. Not so in America.

Also, American life was less formal than in Europe, where people usually observed a code of dress. For instance, I had never seen a woman wear curlers in her hair in a public place. I discovered something else. In Germany, there were three classes of people (upper, middle, lower) and high-class people would not think of having any person who worked for them eat at their table. But here, whenever I would care for a new baby, without exception, I was treated like a member of the family. That would not have happened in the Europe I knew. At first, I was self-conscious, the system was so very different. This, too, is America.

Furthermore, Americans had peculiar ways of decorating their homes. "You wouldn't believe it, but it's true," I wrote to my friends in Germany after I had seen my first American bedroom. "Black wallpaper with birds of paradise, white wall-to-wall carpeting–that's an American bedroom." They wrote back that it was indeed "hard to believe."

* * * * *

In September 1954, near the tenth anniversary of our escape from Cservenka, I found what I had been searching for spiritually. At long, long last, I understood what God wanted from me. Billy Graham was scheduled to speak in Seattle, and Gunther and I went to hear him, parting company when Gunther went to sit with some teenage friends. My English was far from fluent, but the Lord took care of that, for the lady sitting next to me was a Christian who could speak German. She pointed to the text in the German New Testament I had with me and also translated many of Mr. Graham's comments. I liked his apparent sincerity and what he said rang true to me, for he spoke of things I had heard before: the call to repent from sin and live a righteous life out of love for God. "But how, Lord?" my spirit cried out. "I've heard this before. What do you want me to do?"

At that time, Mr. Graham was asking people to "come." That English word I could understand. I had an overwhelming desire to give my life completely to Christ and to live for Him. Now I had an invitation to do something: "Come!" I knew God's Holy Spirit was speaking to me.

"Come, Christine." I recognized His voice. He had directed me in the past from one refugee camp to the other. He had gently wooed me that Christmas Eve in Wiesenthau when He said, "Trust Me, Kristina." It was His peace I had felt in the Armenian village. I even associated Him with the awe-inspiring danger of my hill outside Cservenka. All of these images and impulses seemed to rush together, and the woman next to me must have sensed my yearning, because she turned and said, "Come, don't be shy; I'll go with you."

As we made our way to a special place in front of the platform from which Mr. Graham spoke, I did not see that Gunther was also on his feet. Evidently the message answered what he had been looking for too, and, without noticing each other, Gunther and I together confessed Jesus as Messiah and claimed His promise:

"Everyone therefore who shall confess Me before men, I will also confess him before My Father who is in heaven" (Matt. 10:32). We were also assured of another promise: "He who has the Son has the life; he who does not have the Son of God does not have the life" (1 John 5:12).

I had not known this type of evangelistic gathering in Europe, and I wondered if maybe this was what Pastor Zitt was referring to when shortly before we left Germany he had said, "Christianity is much stronger in America than it is in Europe." Here were adults, some of them weeping unashamedly as they quietly asked God to forgive them and to take control of their lives. We were all reminded that the Bible says we cannot earn salvation, that it is a gift from God which we receive by faith and not by works, a faith like that of Abraham: "And Abraham believed God, and it was reckoned to him as righteousness" (Rom. 4:3). I cried too. My tears were from joy and relief because I now understood that what God wants is for me to acknowledge my total dependence on Him and to quit pretending I am in control. Jesus says, "Come to Me, all who are weary and heavy-laden, and I will give you rest. Take My yoke upon you, and learn from Me, for I am gentle and humble in heart; and you shall find rest for your souls. For My yoke is easy, and My load is light" (Matt. 11:28-30). God's heavy hand lifted from me as I gave Him the load, the load I had been carrying alone for so many years simply because I did not know how to transfer it. The Lord Jesus took my load of guilt when He died in my place on Calvary: "He Himself bore our sins in His body on the cross, that we might die to sin and live to righteousness; for by His wounds you were healed" (1 Pet. 2:24). His eternal life was transferred to me, and His Holy Spirit, the seal of my redemption, now breathes into me the power to live what Jesus demands. What a transaction!

I went home that night a different person, but I did not talk to Karl about what had happened. He was having his own problems adjusting to life in America, particularly in having to start at the bottom of the economic ladder. It would take years of hard work on the part of all of us before we would live anywhere near the level of our former lives in Yugoslavia, yet the dangerous tendency to put money ahead of a right relationship with God was already with us. After what God had done for me in Europe, I did not want to repeat the pattern of the first ten years of my marriage. God had been faithful to me in tight places; I did not want to betray His kindness. Besides, from my own Bible reading, I knew it would be folly to do so. I decided the best role for me was to encourage Karl when he felt despondent and to work whenever I was offered a baby-care job. Karl had never before been in the position of being beholden to anyone and the experience was humbling. Of course he was thankful to be in the United States, but until recent years he had been the one to hire and help others less fortunate as he chose. It was not easy for him to wear the other shoe comfortably.

In 1955 a new pastor came to the Ravenna congregation. Carl and Virginia Anderson quickly became special to our family because they had seven children close in age to our boys and they showed a real affection for Karl and me. Pastor Anderson also encouraged my Christian growth. Once, when he urged me to pray aloud, I hesitated because I did not feel comfortable to pray in English. "Well, then," he said, "pray in German." To pray out loud in a group was a new experience too, and I felt nervous. But the Holy Spirit prayed through me in such a way that the entire congregation said they knew His presence even without understanding all my words. Another time when he was preaching and I happened to be sitting in the second row in plain view of him, he said something in his native Swedish and, believing Swedish and German were very similar, he said, "Now, Mrs. Gegner, you understand what I'm saying, don't you?" I felt flustered because I had no idea what he had said. He must have noticed my embarrassment for he quickly explained the expression himself. We still laugh about the incident, yet under his teaching, my faith and my knowledge of God's word grew up together.

Gunther by now had graduated from high school. Then, with less than a year at the University of Washington, he joined the Army and after serving three years, he and Mary Nolde, a girl from Holland, were married and Gunther began his own business in construction. They became parents of four children: Kenneth, Arlene, David, and Anne Marie.

Kurt, while on a football scholarship at the University of Washington, finished a degree in civil engineering. A couple of his years were important in the annals of Husky football, and Kurt played in the Rose Bowl on New Year's Day 1960 and 1961. Although our finances were still tight, Karl thought these games were important in the life of our son, important enough to borrow the money so we could fly to Pasadena to see Washington win two years in a row. For Kurt, though, the second trip had an exciting prelude: his wedding to Susan Harman took place over Thanksgiving vacation. A year later, on their first anniversary, they became the parents of twin girls, Kathy and Kristi. A third daughter, Andrea, was born five years later. Kurt, having also been part of an ROTC program, spent four years in the Marines.

Norbert followed Kurt with regard to an interest in engineering, but he picked another school, Long Beach State College in California, where he received a degree in electrical engineering. He tried to get into the Air Force so that each brother would serve a different branch of the armed forces, but he was rejected because of his earlier history with asthma. Like Gunther, therefore, he served three years in the Army. He later married a young German woman he had known for many years, Gudrun Box, whose family had run from the Russians in East Germany during World War II. They have two children, Brigitte and Christopher.

In 1966, Karl and I returned to Cservenka for a visit. We made the trip to see relatives still living in Germany and left from Karlsruhe, Germany, by train, traveling through Austria and into Yugoslavia. We arrived in Cservenka early in the morning, and as I walked with Karl along the same streets of my exodus over two decades earlier, I knew the places from road signs only.

We came first to the cemetery, which had become a jungle of uncut grass and weeds. We located the Gegner family tomb and with difficulty restored the marker to an upright position. Apparently nothing had been done in twenty years so that I scarcely recognized my own house. The fence and all trees were gone, as the neighbor I met in Munich after the war had reported. But now stucco was cracked and tiles were either broken or entirely missing from the roof. Streets, too, had gone without repairs. The community was like a ghost town. A Serbian family lived in our place, and they received us graciously. Karl could still speak Serbian and Hungarian, and I could understand much of what was said as the woman showed us, room by room, through the house where my children were born. I cried most of the time, and she responded sympathetically. All my pretty things were gone, and none of the heavy oak furniture remained. Out on the street once more, we walked to the mill and noticed to our dismay that a wing had been burned to the ground and only shabbily replaced. The Lutheran church where I had been confirmed was also burned down. Suddenly Karl took my arm.

"We're being followed. Let's head back to the train station; I want to get out of here as fast as we can."

"Followed! You're imagining things, Karl." I had been aware that the people living in the once-rich German homes were watching from windows, but that was not what Karl was referring to. "Why would anyone follow us?"

"I don't know. But they checked us very closely at the border and asked all kinds of questions about us. I felt uneasy then and from the moment we stepped off the train, that man–there across the street . . . don't look now, but he's the one–has been watching us. I don't want to get stuck here, so let's go."

On the way to the station, we came face to face with a poorly-dressed man who, much to our surprise, almost fell at Karl's feet. "I heard you were in Cservenka, Gegner Karl, so I started to look for you." His eyes were full of tears and his voice quivered. "Why did you leave Cservenka? We didn't hate you. Why did all the German families leave?" Karl tried to soothe him in the Serbian language, and we continued toward the station. "Poor man," Karl said. "He's probably from one of the uneducated families we used to help out with food. He doesn't understand much about politics and war."

We spent only about three hours in Cservenka and boarded the train without incident and headed north to Budapest where Karl's aunt lived. The countryside no longer produced lush crops, and the corn we saw was stunted and sparse. In Budapest, too, we saw how poorly this once-wealthy family now lived under Communism, and we were thankful to be citizens of the United States, living in a free society. When in 1970 we once again visited Germany, the scenes I remembered of Cservenka from four years before blunted any desire to return there.

Following these trips, with our boys married and on their own and with Karl nearing retirement, we settled in the triplex we bought and rented out two units while we lived in one. A predictable pattern returned and for a few years life just went on for Karl and me. This time, though, we did not leave the Lord out. Then, as October 1944 had been one turning point in our lives, so August 1974 would begin another era for me: widowhood. Karl had had one heart attack in 1971, but he recovered and we had no warning on the day of a happy family dinner at our home that death was imminent. He died that night in his sleep. My woes were beginning. Another time of testing had come.

". . . Where is God my Maker,
Who gives songs in the night?' . . ." (Job 35:10)
And He put a new song in my mouth, a song of praise to our God;
Many will see and fear,
And will trust in the LORD. (Psalm 40:3)

Chapter Thirteen

My Certain Refuge

Within two months of Karl's death, Gunther's wife, Mary, began a losing battle with cancer. In the course of her illness, Gunther had one heart attack, but he recovered. When Mary died in September 1976 at the age of thirty-nine, she left four children motherless and my oldest son a widower. The following May, though, we had a wedding, as Gunther married Eunice Wacker, a widow with three children, Preston, Laurie, and Sharie. However, their newly-found happiness was short-lived: that October, Gunther had another heart attack. This time he did not recover and in April 1978—a month before their first wedding anniversary—death claimed him at age forty-two. Eunice was a widow for the second time and with an added responsibility: instead of three children, she had seven. Then in September, a scant five months later, Kurt was suddenly brought low with a rare form of blood cancer, a battle he and the latest in medical technology fought valiantly for almost three years. In June 1980, in the middle of Kurt's trips to the hospital, Gunther's own son, David, age fourteen, was operated on for a brain tumor which had escaped accurate diagnosis for two years. He survived the operation, but on a routine visit a few days later, a shocked Eunice found him dead in his hospital bed. David's death was hard for all of us, but grief fell heaviest on his three surviving siblings, who had lost mother, father, and a brother in less than four years. My own cup of sorrow, moreover, was not yet full. In June 1981, Kurt died at age forty-three.

I reeled from one untimely death to another, barely regaining emotional stability before I plunged again. The certain roadway I had been walking for several years seemed a washout and once more I was groping for something solid to cling to, and I cried out at God. I could understand why God had let me wander during the war in Europe—that was to wake me up to my need of Him. "But why do You take my sons away now, when I trust in You?" I asked repeatedly.

Although with my head I believed God's promise that He would never leave me or forsake me, often times, when I was alone at night, I had little comfort emotionally, and I cried myself weak. Once, after I had returned from a visit to Gunther in the hospital, in anguish I fell to my knees: "O God," I called, "are You really there? If You are there, show me . . . please Lord, . . . please." While I waited in the darkness, the stillness broken only by my sobs, no flashes of light came, no majestic thunder from Heaven filled the room. What slowly came to mind were the words I had heard before: "Come to Me, all who are heavy-laden. Come to Me, and I will give you rest. Come to Me, and you shall find rest for your soul. Come to Me, Christine. Come . . ." Peace from the Lord flooded me, peace that really does pass all understanding, and my sobbing stopped. I slept soundly that night. My sorrow was there, but so was God.

Other nights followed, many of them not filled with peace, when I would beg God to spare my son, all the while heaping blame on myself that poor diets during the war had caused Gunther's heart to deteriorate. During one of these times, I phoned a Christian friend, who asked, "Christine, would you like me to come over?"

"No, don't do that. It's way too late." It must have been eleven o'clock, and, miserable as I was, I did not expect people to drive halfway across the city at that hour. She and her husband came anyway, joining me in my bedroom where I had been crying for hours. They were quick to size up my unhealthy emotional state, and although they cried with me, their counsel did not stop with sympathetic tears. Instead, he opened his Bible to the discussion Jesus had with a grieving Martha before He raised her brother Lazarus from the dead, and read: "I am the resurrection and the life; he who believes in Me shall live even if he dies, and everyone who lives and believes in Me shall never die. Do you believe this?" (John 11:25f).

With Martha, I could answer: "Yes, Lord; I have believed that

You are the Christ, the Son of God, even He who comes into the world" (John 11:27).

"Well, then, Gunther is not a loser. If you really believe what Jesus says, it's impossible to feel bad for Gunther." This Dutch uncle approach surprised me.

"You mean I'm not supposed to cry?" I sputtered. "Gunther is my son!" No, that was not what he meant; Jesus wept at the tomb of Lazarus. But to cry all day long on my bed and not even get dressed, as I had done, was excessive, especially for a Christian who believes that to be absent from the body is to be present with the Lord. Before they left, we prayed together. I think we even sang. There was a cleanness to their sympathy which helped to snap me out of despondency and self-pity. As my griefs piled up, I preferred the strength I got from them to the indulgent outcries of others: "Christine, how can you take all this? I don't see how you can stand it. I don't know what I would do if I were going through what you're going through." I know these people meant well, but their manner always increased my depression.

Losing my sons hurt terribly. It is not the usual order for children to die before their parents, and through it all I gained a Job-like reputation. And, like Job, I had my ups and downs.

"God doesn't hear my prayers; He hasn't answered me," I said on more than one occasion during Kurt's lengthy illness.

"On the contrary, Christine," my firm-spoken friend would reply. And then she would review the ways God had prolonged Kurt's life in answer to very specific prayers. I had to admit that what she said was true.

Over and over I had to be reminded by Christian friends that what life is all about ultimately is to bring glory to God. Prayers for healing, therefore, took this form: "Heal him, Lord, if it will be to Your glory. If healing will not bring praise to Your name, then confirm the promise You made through Paul: 'And we know that God causes all things to work together for good to those who love God, to those who are called according to His purpose'" (Rom. 8:28).

During these personal tragedies, I transferred to another congregation. My good friend Pastor Anderson had retired, and some of my widow friends urged me to attend Christ Church of Northgate, where I met Pastor Dennis Finch. During the many times Pastor Finch prayed for me and my loved ones and drove me to see Kurt, who was hospitalized in another city, neither of us knew how close our paths had come many years earlier.

After Kurt died, I wanted to get away to a whole new setting. Some Christian friends of mine were living temporarily in Norway, and they urged me to visit them there. The spectacular beauty of the countryside together with the blue stillness of Oslofjord was just what I needed for renewal. They also arranged another treat: prior to my flight home, the three of us took a quick trip to southern Germany, a land I never expected to see again, and paid a surprise visit on my sister Anna, my only living sibling. The trip helped me to put events in perspective and quickened my healing process.

Then a few months after my return to Seattle, I learned that Pastor Finch, as a technical sergeant in the Army, had been in Germany with the victorious American forces in the closing days of the war and that he had received the Bronze Star for meritorious service.

"It's what's called a small world, Christine," he said, smiling at my firm-spoken friend and me as we sat around the table having coffee and goodies one afternoon. "I was a secretary with Headquarters 71st Infantry Division, so I rode in a jeep with a colonel who dictated to me in detail what was happening as our troops took town after town. The reports were then sent to the Adjutant General of the United States in Washington, D.C. What you see here," he explained, pointing to some papers he brought with him, "are a few souvenirs I was able to get after the war–copies of memos that describe some of the battles."

Pastor Finch thumbed through the official reports which documented the day-by-day activities of American troops. "Here we are," he said. "It reads that on April 16, 1945, Americans had secured and occupied Bayreuth[5] and that Pegnitz was attacked on April 19."[6]

"Bayreuth? That's only about thirty miles northeast from where I was," I exclaimed. "And Pegnitz was almost due east and closer– about twenty miles according to this map."

"Yes, and after that we moved southeast, toward Austria, taking Amberg, here," he said, pointing once more to the map, "on April 23.[7] We were also cutting off supply routes into Nuremberg along the way. And every day we took growing numbers of German prisoners of war. You must have heard shooting–the Germans put up stiff resistance in that area."

"Yes, I sure did. The earth shook all the time and we really didn't know what to expect from one minute to the next." I told about the incident with the American soldier when troops entered and searched Willersdorf. "On that day, it was beyond my imagination that another American soldier riding in a jeep a few miles from where I stood would one day be my minister!"

We all laughed, and he sampled my chocolate-nut torte. Then he sobered suddenly as he picked up a small booklet.[8]

"Something else that's beyond human imagination is what our men came upon after crossing the Danube River. Near Wels, in Austria, our division liberated a German concentration camp of about 18,000 Jews."

I felt my stomach muscles tighten. "You saw an actual concentration camp?" I asked.

"Yes. As word from our road crews trickled back to headquarters, I rode out to see for myself. We were outraged by what we saw, and I don't think any of us will ever forget the horror of Gunskirchen Lager."

"Jewish people in our town were killed," I told him, "and I saw forced marches and men shot and left beside the road. Then, months later, I heard some ugly rumors circulated by refugees . . . "

"Well, they couldn't have been as ugly as what I saw with my own eyes. Those who died on the way were spared the ultimate in filth, degradation, and brutality." He handed me the booklet which had been written by men in his group. As I slowly turned the pages and saw pictures of the incredible scenes, my eyes fell upon two survivors, young men who could have been among those I had seen.

"We printed that because we didn't want the world to forget what happened," he said.

My friend had been slowly sipping her coffee as she listened. Now she nodded her head solemnly. "I recently met a woman here in Seattle who was in Auschwitz," she said. "I saw the tattooed number and Star of David on her arm, and she told me that she alone of all her family survived; everyone else died in the gas chambers. Yet some people are insisting that the Holocaust never happened!"

"Yes, well, people say lots of things. But I was there too. I saw this myself, and had I not been so thoroughly sickened, I would have gone to Dachau. I spoke with several of the Jews who had been educated in the United States and spoke fluent English. Many from

135

Hungary had been forced to march more that 150 miles over rugged territory and with little food. Thousands died. Nothing in the booklet is exaggerated; words alone, even pictures, can't get at the real horror. When the SS heard the Americans were coming, they deserted the camp, leaving the starving and nearly-crazed inmates without food and water for several days. Then the stronger ones dragged themselves out to the road where our troops first saw them, but others were able to stagger only a few yards before death overtook them. An American officer expressed the sentiment of many when he wrote that the day he saw Gunskirchen Lager was the day he finally knew what he was fighting for, what the war was all about."[9]

"Do you think people living near that camp knew about it?" I asked. I was thinking of the reports about how shocked German citizens had been on hearing about extermination camps.

"No one admitted knowing anything about it, but if you look at the evidence, many people had to know. Gunskirchen Lager was less than four miles from Lambach. You could smell the place when the wind was right. For years, Germans had been conditioned by Hitler's vicious propaganda, and even among those who abhorred his scheme, many nevertheless seared their consciences to the undeniable fact: Jews were being systematically eliminated."

The bluntness of my pastor's words stunned me. We *Volksdeutsche* had also been "conditioned" to believe Hitler.

I was grateful to be spared a reply by the ringing of the telephone. The call was for Pastor Finch, summoning him back to the church office. I think we were all relieved, for the morbid turn in our conversation was not compatible with the good things we were eating. Within a short time, my friend also returned to her home, and I was alone with my thoughts.

* * * * *

Talking about the final days of the war put me in a reflective mood. I looked once more at the booklet left by Pastor Finch. A Jewish rabbi, I read, mustering what little strength remained in his body, clutched the sleeve and kissed the gloved hand of an embarrassed American and then, lifting his face to Heaven, whispered a prayer.[10] I wondered if he had ever asked where God was. So many people, some innocent, some not, and especially Jews, suffered during that war. My mind drifted back over recent years when I had questioned both God's presence and His goodness.

Getting up methodically from the table, I moved to my enclosed sun porch and from the window watched the mellow summer sunlight make strange patterns on the patio below. A beam glanced suddenly off a metallic window sash, and as I closed my eyes against the glare, I stood once more at another window . . . and watched. Refugees were running by the thousands. They knew what they were running from, but they did not know what they were running toward. . . . I then saw myself join the fleeing throngs, not knowing where I was going either. God knew, but it has taken most of my lifetime for Him to work His way with me. . . . A lifetime! I sat motionless for several minutes, my eyes still closed. Then I bowed my head.

"Heavenly Father," I began to pray, "on that day I left Cservenka, You know how much I resented losing my home. But if there had been nothing to disturb my former life and I had been left there stranded in wealth, I probably would have continued to ignore You. Your patience with me is amazing. What I first believed was a disaster, You used . . . to bring me to real life! How can I thank You, Lord? . . . How can I thank You?"

As if in affirmation, I felt the warm sunshine, like God's love, pouring over me. I paused for a time, soaking it up, happy to be in His presence.

"Then in Munich, when I so clearly saw how You led me away from the greater suffering of other *Volksdeutsche*, I remember asking: 'God, what do You have in store for me? Why have you spared me?' It seemed then that You had built a hedge around me, like You did for Job. But You removed Job's hedge and allowed Satan to test him. . . . You took mine away, too. Yet if Job, while in the middle of his suffering, could say, 'Though he slay me, yet will I trust in him' (Job 13:15, KJV), how can I do less? I have an advantage over Job. I know the Umpire and Advocate his faith looked forward to: Christ Jesus. My loved ones won't be replaced as Job's were, but I can praise You for the assurance that all who were taken died in Jesus. I will see them again. And I have my three daughters through marriage, eleven beautiful grandchildren, and one son—I still have Norbert. Thank You, Father."

I felt again Norbert's arms around me as the most recent scene of separation, Kurt's memorial service, pushed into mind. "Don't cry, Mom," he had said softly. "We are the only ones left—we must hold on to each other. I don't want to lose you, too." Years before, when he was little more than a baby, those same arms had gone around my neck and the same "don't cry, Mamma" had been spoken to comfort me. The scene caught me off-guard, and I let the tears run.

"Lord, in my darkest valleys, You never deserted me—I know that now. You kept Your promise . . . You were with me. And, although I still hurt, Your Holy Spirit continues even now to bring me comfort: 'Come to Me, Christine; I have rest for your soul.'

"Yes, LORD, I have come. Help me to keep coming, because there is no other place to go than to You. . . . You are eternal life! No matter how low I was pushed and no matter how deep was my sorrow, You were there. At long last, I know what it is to live in You. My days as a refugee are finished! Accept my thankful praise, . . . accept my love, . . .accept my life, . . . through Christ Jesus my Lord. Amen."

Slowly I raised my head, filled with the overwhelming peace of my Savior and fully assured of the promise:

> The eternal God is thy dwelling place,
> And underneath are the everlasting arms.
> (Deut. 33:27)

ABOUT THE AUTHOR

Frid Eileen Tjorstad was born in Tacoma, Washington, on July 2, 1935, to Robert and Frid Adelaide Tjorstad. Her only sister, Eleanor, was born 4½ years later. Frid's parents had emigrated from Norway, and met and married in the United States.

When Frid was a girl, she loved *The Princess and the Goblin* and *The Princess and Curdie* by George MacDonald. The princess finding her great-great-grandmother at the top of the stairs, and realizing that her grandmother had always been there, knowing her and watching over her, provided a powerful image for Frid of God's loving care. Frid put her faith in Christ as a young girl.

Frid married Hugh Nutley on June 11, 1955. Hugh taught physics and engineering at Seattle Pacific University. They had six children.

Frid completed her college degree in English at SPU in 1972 and an M.A. in English at the UW in 1974. She went on to teach classes part-time at SPU and at Puget Sound College of the Bible and later worked at SPU as the editor of SPU's *Response* magazine from 1977 to 1979. In 1979, Frid resigned as editor of the *Response* to write *Once a Refugee*.

Frid and Hugh had a deep heart for people from other cultures. In the 1970s they sponsored a family fleeing from Vietnam, in 1983 they sponsored a family from Poland who were escaping the Polish government's persecution of the Solidarity Union, and they were active in the 1990s with ministry to international students. They offered free English lessons to these students, followed by a Bible study if they wished.

Hugh died in 2003. Frid continued to be involved with her children and grandchildren and active in her church. After many years of physical and mental decline, on March 30, 2017, Frid went home to be with her Lord and Savior, Jesus Christ.

---

[1] See, on this subject, Raul Hilberg's *The Destruction of the European Jews* (Chicago: Quadrangle Books, 1961), p. 298.

[2] In Anthony Masters's *The Summer That Bled* (London: Michael Joseph Ltd., 1972), the author recounts the heroic yet futile effort by her mother and others to save the life of Hannah Senesh, a young Jewish woman "on trial" in Budapest. On October 13 and 14, Mrs. Senesh, because she spent both days under shelter while Budapest was heavily bombed by the Allies, was unable to plead her daughter's case (p. 282).

[3] Hilberg, pp. 509-513.

[4] II Kings 5:1-14.

[5] From a copy of an official was memorandum dated 21 June 1945 from HEADQUARTERS 71ST INFANTRY DIVISION, APO 360, U. S. ARMY; SUBJECT; Action Against Enemy, Reports After; TO; The Adjutant General, Washington, 25, D.C.; THROUGH; Commanding General, XX Corps, APO 340, U. S. Army. The original was signed by W. G. Wyman, Major General, U. S. Army. This action is described on p. 6.

[6] Ibid., p. 8.

[7] Ibid., p. 9.

[8] "Gunskirchen Lager" is a compilation of eyewitnesses' accounts, photographs, and sketches. The cover of Mr. Finch's copy is missing, but in the foreword Major General Willard G. Wyman writes: "This is a true record. I saw Gunskirchen Lager myself . . .": (p. 3). Other copy reads: "In order that more people may know about the record of German inhumanity and barbarity revealed at Gunskirchen, the 71st Division publishes this booklet" (p. 12).

[9] Ibid., p. 11.

[10] Ibid., p. 20.

All Scripture is quoted from the New American Standard Bible except where designated KJV (King James Version).

Made in the USA
Lexington, KY
27 July 2018